PROMOTING YOUR BUSINESS

How to Harness the Power of Media Relations and Influencer Marketing

BRANT SKOGRAND, APR, MBC, CPPM

WITH KATE MAKOWSKI AND ALIKI VROHIDIS

www.skograndpr.com

Copyright © 2019 Brant Skogrand, Kate Makowski and Aliki Vrohidis

All rights reserved.

ISBN: 978-1-704-82700-1

DEDICATION

Brant would like to thank Carol Pine and Marcia Appel, the mentors who launched his public relations career.

Kate would like to dedicate her contribution to the book to her parents for helping her discover her love of strategic communications!

Aliki dedicates this book to her mom, Deb. Thank you for your unwavering support.

OTHER BOOKS BY BRANT SKOGRAND

- Maynard's Memories: Life Lessons from the Developer of Airlake Industrial Park in Lakeville, Minnesota
- 19 Tips for Successful Public Relations: Insights on Media Relations and Reputation Management
- From Fringe Party to Serious Contender: An Analysis of Green Party of Minnesota Communications

Get in touch with us! Visit www.skograndpr.com.

PROMOTING YOUR BUSINESS

Copyright © 2019 by Brant Skogrand, Kate Makowski and Aliki Vrohidis.

All rights reserved. No portion of this book may be reproduced, stored in a retrieval system, or transmitted in any form or by any means – electronic, mechanical, photocopy, recording, or any other – except for brief quotation in printed reviews, without the prior permission of the publisher.

Published by:
Skogrand PR Solutions, LLC
7131 159th Street West
Apple Valley, MN 55124

CONTENTS

Introduction   xiii

PART ONE
MEDIA RELATIONS 101

Benefits of media coverage   2

When to do media relations overview   4

When to do media relations: company announcement   6

When to do media relations: promoting an event   8

When to do media relations: trending news stories   10

When to do media relations: tell the big picture   12

When to do media relations: media coverage opportunities   14

What makes something newsworthy   16

Public relations plan elements	18
What is a press release?	21
How to write a fact sheet	28
Understanding the basics of SEO for public relations	32
Business Wire releases "A Guide to Press Release Optimization"	36
How to find media contact information	38
Understanding media lead times	40
Where to send press releases	42
Determining press release distribution	44
Don't stop using the phone: the importance of follow-up calls	46
Preparing for a newspaper or magazine interview	48
TV interview tips	50
Radio interview tips	52

What to do when a reporter calls	54
How to leverage media coverage	56
Church public relations	58
Changes and constants in media relations	60

PART TWO
MEDIA RELATIONS 201

How to build relationships with reporters	63
Beyond the press release: developing other media materials	65
When to hold a press conference	70
The value of a MAT release	72
Thought leadership via bylined articles	74
Optimizing your online pressroom	77
Company name changes	82
Coordinating a successful media tour	84

Developing an expert source relationship

with the media	86
Landing a media briefing	88
Using research for publicity's sake	90
What to do if "The Lookout" shows up	93
The art of the apology	95
Effective crisis communication	96
What does a PR professional do?	98
When to hire a PR firm	100
How to find a public relations firm	102
Measuring media relations success	104

PART THREE
LET'S HEAR FROM THE JOURNALISTS AND INFLUENCERS

Twin Cities journalists address changing landscape	108
Why influencer marketing is important	111

Influencer marketing best practices	113
Brands that have succeeded with influencer marketing	116
Meet an influencer: Bruno Bornsztein	119
Meet the media: Bill Sherck	124
Nontraditional media panel reveals many similarities	130
Engaging the media in a digital world	132
Meet the media: Josh Rosenthal	136
Social news gathering	140
Meet the media: Bill Hudson, Stephanie March and Thomas Lee	142
A pleasant Minnesota surprise for PRWeek editor-in-chief	144

PART FOUR
PUBLIC RELATIONS CASE STUDIES

Tylenol	148
Nestlé infant formula	151
Target data breach	153
Toxic Shock Syndrome	156
Chipotle E. coli and norovirus outbreak	160

INTRODUCTION

At its core, public relations is about two-way communication that's mutually beneficial.

There are many aspects to public relations, including: media relations, influencer marketing, crisis communications, social media, internal communications and more.

Thanks to the visibility it can create, media relations is often considered the most well-known aspect.

In this book, I, along with former Skogrand PR Solutions interns Kate Makowski and Aliki Vrohidis, demystify media relations. You'll learn the basics as well as more advanced media relations tactics.

We also dive into influencer marketing. You'll hear straight from journalists and influencers on their wants and needs.

In the Public Relations Case Studies section, you'll learn by example which brands handled a crisis well and which ones failed.

If done right, public relations can have a tremendous impact on your organization.

Here's to your success!

Brant Skogrand, November 2019

PART ONE
MEDIA RELATIONS 101

BENEFITS OF MEDIA COVERAGE

Despite the fragmented nature in which people receive information today, there's still value in using media relations to secure a positive story in traditional media outlets.

Some of the benefits of media coverage on a TV or radio station, or in a newspaper or magazine include:

- **Visibility.** In our hometown of Minneapolis, the Star Tribune has a circulation of nearly 300,000. On Sundays, close to 400,000 people read the Star Tribune. Land a story in USA Today or The Wall Street Journal, and millions of eyeballs will see you.

- **Third-party credibility.** According to Pew Research Center,[1] local daily newspapers and local TV news still rank high in believability despite declines in credibility for some national news organizations. Also, information from the press[2] is trusted more than government and business sources. Consumers generally know that media outlets typically have an editorial process. If a reporter writes a positive story about your company, it's more credible than you running an advertisement touting how great your organization is.

- **Reduced barriers to entry.** We, just like any consumer, need to hear a company name or message several times before it sinks in. By obtaining media coverage in numerous outlets that connect with your target audience, hopefully consumers will think of your organization when they are in the market for your product or service.

- **Assistance in achieving business goals.** This is the reason to start media relations in the first place. Positive media coverage is an integral part of a marketing campaign and can help to drive product sales, increased enrollment, or whatever your business goal might be.

After obtaining media coverage, leverage it by posting links on your social media sites, sharing the story with employees, sending reprints as direct mail pieces to customers and prospects, etc. — you have earned it!

WHEN TO DO MEDIA RELATIONS OVERVIEW

Now that you know the benefits of media coverage, it's important to understand know when to do media relations.

Think about the types of news stories that you see in the media, and you'll get a good idea.

A company announcement is an excellent reason to reach out to the media. Perhaps your organization is launching a new product. Maybe your company has hired a new executive or promoted someone to the executive suite. Possibly your company is purchasing another company or is being acquired.

Events can be another time to do media relations. In this instance, something that appeals to the general public, like a store opening or an in-store celebrity autograph signing, would be appropriate to promote. The media won't be interested in your customer appreciation event, so don't waste their time on that.

If your organization is in the know on trends, that might be a good time to pitch the media. Perhaps your company is in residential real estate and has the pulse on which neighborhoods are hot in your market. Or maybe you work for a clothing retailer and know what tweens are buying today.

If your organization is part of a bigger story, take the time to pitch the media. News organizations are often interested in the local angle. For example, with the number of states legalizing recreational marijuana, the media would be interested if your company has some connection.

To think of additional coverage opportunities for your organization, try to get into the mindset of a reporter. What is the local angle? Is there a celebrity involved? Is there a great human interest story? Is there something unique happening? Is your organization doing something to help alleviate a tragic situation?

WHEN TO DO MEDIA RELATIONS: COMPANY ANNOUNCEMENT

The first important time to do media relations is during a company announcement. If your company is looking for media attention, note that major company changes or interesting updates are prime opportunities for gathering that coverage. Some examples of a company announcement include: product launches, new hires, promotions and acquisitions.

The iPhone 7 was one of the most highly anticipated technology updates of the year (or the past couple of years, if we're being honest) when it came out in 2016. Although Apple probably doesn't rely on spectacular media coverage to solidify sales or make sure that their product launch is known, the iPhone 7 reveal is a great example of a product launch or company announcement that would warrant a reason to seek media coverage. Quick: Do a Google search for the iPhone 7, and scroll through the search results. Media love to use new products as a vehicle for compare and contrast articles, product reviews, and industry insights. On June 3, 2016, Forbes posted an article titled, "The iPhone 7: Five Reasons I Would and Wouldn't Buy It."[1]

Publications like Forbes benefit from articles like this, as they have attained valuable new insights on desired products that consumers want to know.

This sentiment doesn't just apply to Apple. When you pitch reporters on a new and exciting company announcement, you provide them with coveted information they need to get readers. Many companies devote complete articles or sections to new hire and promotion articles. The Minnesota Business magazine and the Star Tribune Movers & Shakers are a couple examples of this. If you're looking to hear back from the media, providing an announcement with industry knowledge is a great time to do media relations.

WHEN TO DO MEDIA RELATIONS: PROMOTING AN EVENT

Oftentimes, you and your company are not just looking for online engagements – you are also looking for (and promoting) opportunities to meet your customers. Whether you are sponsoring an event or hosting an event yourself, most likely you have an end goal of increasing attendance and awareness. That's why events are an ideal subject for media, as they are a two-for-one: brand awareness and driving more people to your event.

For nonprofit or charitable organizations, event coverage is traditional and incredibly necessary. Walks for awareness of diseases or illnesses, donation roundups, and events of the like are great topics of discussion for media outlets to cover. It gives them the opportunity to promote the event before it happens, and also the opportunity to attend and cover the event live. This is important, because video and livestreaming is so relevant in our current social and professional media world. The value of being at an event and recording it while it is in progress is invaluable to viewers.

In April 2016, the American Cancer Society (ACS) hosted its second Relay for Life in Minneapolis. Major Twin Cities networks like KARE11 covered and promoted the relay before it took place.

In the article and video clip that KARE11 published,[1] the station gave background information on the ACS and how viewers could get involved. The ACS gained coverage again (later in the year) with the Relay for Life Global Celebration that took place at the Mall of America. Media want to cover big, charitable events. You provide them with content that elicits goodwill from viewers, and they boost your chance of donors or event-goers.

Other types of events make great opportunities for media coverage, too. If you are a theater company, you can pitch your upcoming show dates to local media. Perhaps you are on the planning committee for a city festival, or maybe your company's anniversary is fast approaching and your boss is throwing a picnic. Events are off the daily beaten path, and the more unique your event is, the better chance you have of attaining media coverage. When you pitch to the media about your company event, you give them the chance to stimulate community involvement. Events are an appropriate and exciting time to invest in media relations.

WHEN TO DO MEDIA RELATIONS: TRENDING NEWS STORIES

Much of what goes into news coverage is popularity and relevance. The media covers what people want to hear about and what is popular at the time, whether it's pop culture, sports or crazy weather. The topic of popularity appropriately leads us into another time to do media relations: when something is trending.

What does it mean if something is trending? You probably know by now. If a subject is trending, it is currently among the most popular topics of the area to which it is trending. A good way to activate media coverage is to prioritize pitching during the time when what you're pitching is trending or is related to trending news stories.

Media surrounding presidential elections floods, and has flooded, our newsfeeds and media outlets. Some companies (completely unrelated to politics) jumped on the political posting bandwagon during the 2016 election and earned some attention for doing so. After the Washington Post leaked the video of Donald Trump bragging about sexually assaulting women, Tic Tac tweeted an opinion on the matter: "Tic Tac respects all women. We find the recent statements and behavior completely inappropriate and unacceptable."[1]

Then, people started talking about Tic Tac. In fact, a lot of people did, including Buzzfeed,[2] Adweek and Cosmopolitan, to name just a few. From fewer than 140 characters, Tic Tac had sold itself to handfuls of big-name media outlets and gained almost instant media coverage (and lots of it). The driving point to take from this example is that Tic Tac saw what was trending in the rest of the world and did something about it. Tic Tac is not a company that had an immediate stake in the presidential election. They are not a politically charged company (until then, at least). However, none of these facts stopped them from attaining media coverage by following trending news stories.

WHEN TO DO MEDIA RELATIONS: TELL THE BIG PICTURE

Big news about what's happening in the world is ever one-dimensional. When something "big" happens, there are many stakeholders involved. If there is a tragedy, say for example a hurricane, media don't just livestream the bad weather. Reporters interview those who lost homes or who were injured, those who have family who lost homes or were injured, political leaders, weather experts, and many others. Newspeople understand that all of these smaller coverages are puzzle pieces that contribute to a bigger story. This is the next important time to do media relations: when you have information that helps tell the big picture.

In 2013, the Minneapolis/St. Paul Business Journal[1] wrote an article on Glam Doll Donuts and their large stock of Sriracha. Glam Doll Donuts is a local Minnesota donut shop with a spectacular reputation. In the article, it's explained that Huy Fong Foods Inc. (was) going through a dispute that possibly would've shut down hot sauce production. Co-owner of Glam Doll Donuts Teresa Fox consequently bought a mass quantity of Sriracha hot sauce, in order to ensure that the shop would have enough Sriracha for its spicy peanut butter donut, the "Chart Topper."

Fox's story is not the main event. Ultimately, people were more concerned about the outcome of Huy Fong Foods Inc. more than they were worried for a spicy donut from Minneapolis. However, Fox's story adds another layer to Sriracha's dispute. It thickens the plot, and pulls in more readers. It's also smart because typically you wouldn't consider hot sauce as newsworthy information. If your company is acting or reacting to current events, possibly you have information that could help tell the big picture. When you have a piece of this puzzle, it is time to initiate media relations.

WHEN TO DO MEDIA RELATIONS: MEDIA COVERAGE OPPORTUNITIES

You have read that there are specific instances when media relations can and should be implemented; however, there are endless opportunities for media relations to be applied! Opportunities include local news, celebrity updates, general or unique human interests, tragedies and more.

Let's revisit Glam Doll Donuts, the local Minnesota bakery that featured in Minneapolis/St. Paul Business Journal in 2013 for their "tasty spin" on a traditional bakery item. If your company offers a unique product, you can give reporters an opportunity to try it, rank it, or publicize how it's disrupting the norms of the industry.

Halo Top ice cream, a healthy dessert rising in popularity due to its great taste and low calories, received similar press to Glam Doll Donuts. Foodbeast covered Halo Top products and detailed its unique blend of low calories and thick, rich ice cream qualities. Buzzfeed has also covered Halo Top and compared it to other ice cream brands like Arctic Zero and Häagen-Dazs.[1] Halo Top didn't have an event to publicize or a company announcement; they had a product that stood out amongst its competitors and media personnel who saw the value in its uniqueness.

Keep an eye out and an ear open in your office space. Stay up to date with your industry for opportunities to get media coverage.

WHAT MAKES SOMETHING NEWSWORTHY

In my work with clients, I (Brant) always try to find the newsworthy aspects of the information that they want to announce.

To assist them in understanding what makes something newsworthy, it helps to take the viewpoint of a news reporter or editor.

I found the following news values list from the University of Utah very useful:

1. **Impact:** The significance, importance or consequence of an event or trend; the greater the consequence, and the larger the number of people for whom an event is important the greater the newsworthiness.
2. **Timeliness:** The more recent, the more newsworthy. In some cases, timeliness is relative. An event may have occurred in the past but only have been learned about recently.
3. **Prominence:** Occurrences featuring well-known individuals or institutions are newsworthy. Well-knownness may spring either from the power the person or institution possesses – the president, the

speaker of the House of Representatives – or from celebrity – the late Princess Diana or fashion designer Gianni Versace.
4. **Proximity:** Closeness of the occurrence to the audience may be gauged either geographically – close by events, all other things being equal, are more important than distant ones – or in terms of the assumed values, interest and expectations of the news audience.
5. **The bizarre:** The unusual, unorthodox, or unexpected attracts attention. Boxer Mike Tyson's disqualification for biting off a piece of Evander Holyfield's ear moves the story from the sports pages and the end of a newscast to the front pages and the top of the newscast.
6. **Conflict:** Controversy and open clashes are newsworthy, inviting attention on their own, almost regardless of what the conflict is over. Conflict reveals underlying causes of disagreement between individuals and institutions in a society.
7. **Currency:** Occasionally something becomes an idea whose time has come. The matter assumes a life of its own, and for a time assumes momentum in news reportage.
8. **Human interest:** Those stories that have more of an entertainment factor versus any of the above – not that some of the other news values cannot have an entertainment value.

Consider these news values the next time you're trying to determine the appropriate pitch to a reporter.

In addition, issue your news on your owned media channels (newsroom on your website, social media, etc.) first. If a topic gains traction there, share statistics, such as social media likes or shares, in your pitch. That will help your contacts at media outlets determine if there is broad interest in the topic.

PUBLIC RELATIONS PLAN ELEMENTS

Just like many aspects of business (and life in general), a public relations program works best when it is planned out. One way to describe the public relations process is RACE, an acronym coined by John Marston in his book "The Nature of Public Relations." RACE describes the four elements of public relations:

- Research – What is the problem or situation?
- Action (program planning) – What is going to be done about it?
- Communication (execution) – How will the public be told?
- Evaluation – Was the audience reached and what was the effect?

A public relations plan provides a framework for a campaign. According to the book "Public Relations: Strategies and Tactics" (Wilcox, Ault, Agee and Cameron), a public relations plan includes the following elements:

- Situation
- Objectives
- Audience
- Strategy

- Tactics
- Calendar/Timetable
- Budget
- Evaluation

Let's look at each of these elements individually.

Situation. This element provides a brief overview of the public relations plan and why it was needed in the first place. A quick summary of any research related to the public relations plan is appropriate in this section as well.

Objectives. In general, objectives fall into two categories: informational and motivational. Informational objectives generally focus on an increase in public awareness and/or delivery of key messages, while motivational objectives relate to quantifiable measures such as an increase in sales. One example of an informational objective from my (Brant) work with Thrivent Financial was "Raise Thrivent Financial's visibility in the investments industry as a means of attracting top talent."

Audience. The best approach is to have a specific audience, such as one based on age, geography, gender, etc.

Strategy. The strategy section of a public relations plan describes how the objectives are going to be achieved. This element of the plan also should include the key themes or messages of the campaign. An example of a strategy from the Thrivent Financial plan was "Highlight the organization's consistent, competitive performance to media."

Tactics. This section outlines the day-to-day actions that will activate the strategies in order to achieve the objectives. Each strategy often has several tactics supporting it. Examples of tactics range from press releases to media tours to press conferences and more.

Calendar/Timetable. Not only is it important to outline when a public relations campaign will take place, it also is vital to determine the sequence of activities and a calendar of when the specific tactics and steps need to happen.

Budget. A budget can provide an overall total for the campaign and/or a breakdown of budget items for each of the campaign components. Budgets are often divided into staff time and out-of-pocket expenses (wire services, mileage, etc.).

Evaluation. This is the "E" in RACE. This section ties back to the objectives to see if they were achieved at the end of the public relations campaign.

Having a public relations plan provides an excellent overview of a public relations campaign and is very useful along the way to mark progress in a campaign. A plan also helps everyone involved understand the big picture.

WHAT IS A PRESS RELEASE?

There are several tools and tactics that can be used to communicate an organization's news to the media. One of the most popular methods is the press release (also known as a news release). To provide a concrete example, below is a press release that I (Brant) wrote and distributed when I worked for a company called West (https://legal.thomsonreuters.com/en). Let's take a look at some of the key elements of a press release:

1. **Company information:** The company name, address, phone number and website URL let journalists know who is sending the information.
2. **Media contact:** Journalists need to know whom to contact for more information or to request an interview. Often the media contact is the person who wrote the press release, but it's more important for the contact to be someone whom journalists can get in touch with quickly if they would like to do a story.
3. **Headline:** Summarizes the essence of the story; Ann Wylie, a highly respected communications professional, recommends that the headline be eight words or fewer.
4. **Subhead/deck:** Provides an opportunity to expand a bit upon the headline while still providing a summary. Wylie recommends that the deck be 14 words or fewer.

5. **Dateline:** Includes information on the city and state the information is originating from as well as the date of release.
6. **Body:** This is the essence of the news release, and includes more details about the announcement, quotes from appropriate people, etc. When writing the body, try to think like a journalist. Consider what will be most interesting to a media outlet's audience (the news hook). Given that many media outlets are doing more with less, there's a distinct possibility that your press release could be used verbatim.
7. **Boilerplate:** Offers a summary of the organization issuing the press release, such as services offered, ticker symbol, key statistics, etc.
8. **Close:** Lets the journalist know that this is the end of the press release; typically "###" or "-30-". Also, in case the pages get separated, it's important to include "2 of 3" or the respective number of pages.

West
610 Opperman Drive
Eagan, MN 55123
Tel (651) 687-7000
www.westgroup.com

News Release

Media Contact:
Brant Skogrand, APR
West
651.848.8578
brant.skogrand@westgroup.com

For Immediate Release

West Announces Westlaw Litigator

New Powerful Tools for Litigators to Evaluate, Investigate and Profile Attorneys and Experts

EAGAN, Minn., February 17, 2003 – Competition is forcing law firms to be more productive and selective in the cases that they take on. To assist legal professionals with their litigation work, West is launching Westlaw Litigator, an offering that delivers powerful tools to: help legal professionals determine the value of a case; investigate parties, opposing counsel and expert witnesses; learn how judges have ruled on similar legal issues; and develop more sophisticated strategies for trial.

Case evaluation and trial preparation can be a burdensome process. Litigators need a tremendous amount of information, including jury verdicts, local court rules, trial court documents, jury instructions, depositions, trial transcripts and more. Unfortunately, this information can be difficult or impossible to find. With Westlaw Litigator, critical information that attorneys need to prepare for trial is available in one place at their fingertips – on the new Litigation tab on Westlaw®.

"Westlaw Litigator provides a comprehensive one-stop research tool for legal professionals," said Mike Wilens, West president. "Litigators spend most of their time preparing for trial, and Westlaw Litigator gives them the opportunity to complete pretrial preparation faster, easier and with more confidence."

Attorneys will find Westlaw Litigator particularly useful for many common litigation tasks such as valuing a case, finding an expert witness, investigating parties, profiling opposing counsel and developing a trial strategy. In addition, West is integrating jury verdicts, dockets, local court rules, trial court documents, jury instructions, depositions and trial transcripts with its comprehensive appellate case collection, providing more and better information for litigators.

"Westlaw Litigator brings trusted content together in ways like never before," said Erv Barbre, senior vice president, New Product Development for West. "Legal professionals now have new ways to find and analyze data, resulting in significant competitive advantages."

West also is offering 22 state Westlaw Litigator products covering 24 jurisdictions: Alabama, California, Colorado, District of Columbia Area (Washington, D.C., Maryland and Virginia), Florida, Georgia, Illinois, Louisiana, Massachusetts, Michigan, Minnesota, Missouri, Mississippi, New Jersey, New York, Ohio, Oklahoma, Pennsylvania, South Carolina, Tennessee, Texas and Washington.

Westlaw Litigator enables litigators to use the technology that they are already familiar with and prefer to prepare for trial – Westlaw.

For more information or a demonstration of the product, go to www.westlawlitigator.com.

About West
Headquartered in Eagan, Minn., West is the foremost provider of integrated information solutions to the U.S. legal market. West is a business within The Thomson Corporation (NYSE: TOC; TSX: TOC) and was formed when West Publishing and Thomson Legal Publishing merged in June 1996. For more information, please visit the West Web site at www.westgroup.com.

About The Thomson Corporation

The Thomson Corporation (http://www.thomson.com), with 2001 revenues of $7.2 billion, is a global leader in providing integrated information solutions to business and professional customers. Thomson provides value-added information, software applications and tools to more than 20 million users in the fields of law, tax, accounting, financial services, higher education, reference information, corporate training and assessment, scientific research and healthcare. The Corporation's common shares are listed on the New York and Toronto stock exchanges (NYSE: TOC; TSX: TOC).

###

A related tactic used to announce information – generally events – to the media is called a media advisory. Below is an example from my days at Musicland Stores Corporation.

Let's take a look at the key elements of a media advisory:

1. **Contact information:** it's important for reporters to know whom to contact if they want more information or need credentials to cover an event.
2. **Headline:** again, a pithy summary is best.
3. **Facts:** this is the essence of the media advisory, answering the core questions that reporters have about an event and why it is newsworthy.
4. **Boilerplate:** offers a summary of the organization issuing the media advisory, such as services offered, ticker symbol, key statistics, etc.

In general, media advisories should be limited to one page to make it easier for reporters to capture the essence of an event – the purpose of a media advisory is to get the reporter to attend the event in person.

For More Information:
Brant Skogrand
(612) 931-8325
bskogrand@musicland.com

MEDIA ADVISORY/PHOTO OPPORTUNITY

Sam Goody Rocks Mall of America with Def Leppard

WHAT: Rockers Def Leppard will greet fans and sign autographs at the Mall of America Rotunda.

WHO: Promoting their ninth album, "Euphoria," Def Leppard will appear at Mall of America to sign autographs for their fans. The band will sign as many autographs as time allows between noon and 2 p.m. "Euphoria," already gold in the United States, debuted at number 11 on the Billboard charts and features the hit single "Promises."

After selling 15 million copies of their 1987 release, "Hysteria," Def Leppard has continued through the years to produce other world-renowned albums with hits that include "Let's Get Rocked" and "Pour Some Sugar On Me." The Island Def Jam Music Group, Sam Goody and Mall of America are sponsoring the event.

WHEN: Noon to 2 p.m. Sunday, September 12

WHERE: Mall of America Rotunda
356 North Garden
Bloomington, MN 55425
(612) 851-0707

Sam Goody is a division of Musicland Stores Corporation (NYSE:MLG). Based in Minneapolis, Musicland Stores Corporation is the leading specialty retailer of home-entertainment software products in the United States. As of June 30, 1999, the company operated 1,325 retail stores in 49 states, Puerto Rico and the Virgin Islands under the names Sam Goody, Suncoast Motion Picture Company, Media Play and On Cue. In addition to its four store formats, Musicland also operates five commercial Web sites including: SamGoody.com (http://www.samgoody.com), Suncoast.com, MediaPlay.com, OnCue.com and Requestline.com. For additional information on Musicland Stores Corporation, visit the company's Web site at http://www.musicland.com.

HOW TO WRITE A FACT SHEET

As the media are constantly on deadline, it's imperative to have materials about your client or organization ready ahead of media outreach. One type of document to have ready is a PR fact sheet. To that end, here are some insights on how to write a fact sheet.

A PR fact sheet typically is one to two pages long and includes the following types of information about your client or organization:

- Founding date
- Number of employees
- Executive leadership
- Overview of product or service
- Audiences for which the product or service is most useful
- Key client industries
- Current topics in the industry
- Other facts that the media might find relevant

Here's a fact sheet example for a Skogrand PR Solutions client, Fiscal Advantage — and its software program, Fiscal Checkup.

Fiscal Advantage Corporate Backgrounder

- Fiscal Advantage was conceptualized in 2008 by VP of Business Development Daniel O'Connell
- CEO Roger Jacobi joined the company in 2015
- The software, Fiscal Checkup (www.fiscalcheckup.com), was launched in May 2015
- Located in Lake Elmo, Minn.
- Four employees

Service or Product Information Overview

Fiscal Checkup is a web-based software platform designed to help small- to medium-sized companies get actionable data out of their financial statements. Whether it's creating a larger return on investments or small business improvements, Fiscal Advantage helps organizations with:

- Improving fiscal health and maximizing enterprise value
- Customizable and comprehensive financial analysis
- Detailed reports that provide valuable insights
- Analyzing large sets of data
- Understandable, detailed reports regarding company opportunities.

Fiscal Checkup delivers six customized, printable reports:

- **Executive summary:** A top-level analysis of the company's financial data using easy-to-understand charts and graphs that includes recommendations for improvements and an estimate value of the business. Included in the Executive Summary is a Forecasting tool where companies can get tremendous insight

on the seven major inputs that identifies future profits, cash needs, collateral analysis and the company's bankability.
- **Industry comparables chart:** The most comprehensive industry comparison available, using up to five NAIC codes and qualitative data provided about the company and its markets. When benchmarking an industry, Fiscal Checkup uniquely provides and exact industry replica of a business. Without that, you are comparing apples to oranges.
- **Business valuation:** A sophisticated, financial-driven valuation of the business to use as a tool to understand the value components of the enterprise and how improvements impact future value. Fiscal Checkup gains insight with subjective information that relates to value. Sophisticated analytics and a market perspective drives an informative valuation.
- **Cash driver report:** An analysis of the company's cash management (A/R, A/P, inventory, the cash conversion cycle and industry comparison) to evaluate the short-term assets and identify areas for cash flow improvement.
- **Profit driver report:** An analysis of COGS and operating expenses, comparing the company's performance to industry data to improve profitability, growth and enterprise value. Includes a discussion of capital expenditures and a sales-centric review of the market and company dynamics.
- **Lenders report:** A detailed compilation of income statements, balance sheets, cash contribution analysis which compares historic versus new sales, ratio review, abbreviated industry comparables report and Uniform Credit Analysis (UCA) cash flow statement as well an objective risk rating analysis that lenders use when reviewing loan requests. This report gives companies a good banking perspective of their business.

Most Useful For:

- CEO of a company with $1 to $30 million in revenue
- CFO of a company with $10 to $200 million in revenue
- CPA
- Consultant to small- to medium-sized companies

Key Industries

- Manufacturing
- Accounting
- Retail
- Consulting
- Services

Current Topics in the Industry

- Mergers/acquisitions
- Business valuation
- Cash flow improvement
- Performance benchmarking
- Increasing profits

UNDERSTANDING THE BASICS OF SEO FOR PUBLIC RELATIONS

Search engine optimization (SEO) is a discipline that public relations professionals should have some awareness of.

SEO has a strong intersection with public relations and social media, given the importance of online presence to brands. If SEO is new to you, this overview will be helpful.

Search engine optimization definition

According to **Search Engine Wiki**, SEO is "the use of search engines to draw traffic to a website. It's the technique of attaining a higher ranking in search engines and directories via alteration of website code and copy to make it more search engine compatible."

SEO is important because 75 percent of users never scroll past the first page of search results.[1] I know that's generally the case with me (Brant). If I'm really digging for something, I'll go all the way to page four.

Keyword research

Keywords are the most crucial element to SEO. Search engines work to match queries that have appropriate keywords in them with the most relevant content on the Internet.

Keywords are phrases you wish to target. They are the terms that potential website visitors would use in search engines. As an example, think about what you would type into Google to find an excellent Italian restaurant in the Twin Cities. You might type in "Italian restaurant Minneapolis," "Italian restaurant St. Paul," "best Italian restaurant Twin Cities," or "best Italian restaurant Minneapolis St. Paul."

To come up with relevant keywords for your project, think about your target market. Is there a specific geography, age or gender with which you want to connect?

Write down as many keywords as you can think of, and then do some research to find out how frequently they actually are used. Some tools to determine how popular keywords are include: **Google Ads**, **SEMrush** and **Raven Tools**.

Optimizing press releases

Like it or not, search engines don't have a sense of humor, and that impacts how clever one can make the headlines and copy in a press release. One aspect of effectively optimizing a press release going out on a wire service (Business Wire, PR Newswire, etc.) is to use a clear (not necessarily clever) headline. Another important tip to take into account is to place your key messages at the beginning of the press release, as search engines consider the copy near the beginning of the release more important than the rest of the copy.

To use the most appropriate number of characters for readers (and online news services like Google News), noted writing expert **Ann Wylie** recommends keeping the headline length to eight words or fewer, the deck/subhead length to 14 words or fewer, and the lead paragraph to 25 words or fewer.

Now back to the relevant keywords. Hyperlinks to the respective page on your organization's website are important to the algorithms of search engines.

The keywords that you consider important should be hyperlinked in your press release, but use caution. Yahoo! Finance, one of the leading Internet news sites, has placed restrictions on hyperlinks in a press release, such as: one hyperlink per every 100 words, a maximum of six links within a press release, and a maximum of three consecutive words can be hyperlinked.

Using photos for SEO opportunities

Search engines are visually impaired, which is why keywords are so important. Search engines can read the words on a page, but not see photos.

However, a related way that search engines can "see" photos is the associated text that can be assigned to each photo. In a press release, the associated text comes into play when publishing a multimedia press release using a wire service. Remember to use the keywords that you deemed relevant.

Understanding META tags

META tags are HTML tags that are in the code of a website. I mention them here just because they are important to SEO, and you see them every day in search engines.

> Secure File Sharing and Email, Private Cloud | **Sparkweave**, LLC
> www.**sparkweave**.com/ ▾
> **Sparkweave** provides enterprises with secure file sharing and sync, secure email service, and a private cloud platform. Start your 30-day trial today.
> Syncweave - Partners - Fileweave - Mailweave

In the example above for **Sparkweave** (a client that Brant worked with through **KC Associates**), the TITLE tag is the top line, and the META description is the phrase that starts with "Sparkweave" and ends with "today." Other aspects of META tags include the keywords tag and ALT IMG/associated text for images. (The keywords tag and the ALT IMG/associated text don't show up in search engine results, but are in the HTML code.)

Optimizing your online pressroom

Having a pressroom that is very easy for journalists to find and has the information that they need can make the difference between your organization making the cut in a news story or not.

In research that Brant conducted with journalists for an article he co-wrote for TACTICS,[2] he found:

- Keep it simple.
- Make media contact information prominent.
- Ensure easy access from your company's home page.
- Provide RSS feeds.
- Keep your online pressroom organized.
- Use the terms "media" and "press" in your online pressroom.
- Offer a search box.
- Provide more than just press releases.

BUSINESS WIRE RELEASES 'A GUIDE TO PRESS RELEASE OPTIMIZATION'

Major changes in search algorithms over the years have kept search engine optimizers and public relations professionals on their toes.

Press releases, a key tactic in a public relations professional's toolkit, can have an impact on SEO if done correctly. To advise the public relations, investor relations and communications industries, Business Wire issued a guidance report titled "A Guide for Press Release Optimization."

"In recent years we have seen many press releases more focused on SEO keywords and strategically placed links — at the expense of quality content. Our new research report provides a welcome path for PR practitioners to return their focus on quality writing. Well-written press releases with engaging multimedia content continue to be among the most powerful and cost-effective communications tools available. We are thrilled to see that quality writing and quality content are at the top of PR best practices for SEO in 2014," said Tom Becktold, senior vice president of marketing for Business Wire.

The report offers the following 10 tips:

1. Research and learn "real time" user behavior
2. Make friends with the algorithms
3. Make format improvements
4. Use natural links
5. Press release keywords
6. Focus on quality content
7. Always include multimedia
8. Use social media strategically
9. Use responsive design for mobile
10. Choose the proper distribution method

HOW TO FIND MEDIA CONTACT INFORMATION

While reporters are eager to get the latest scoop, they also are awfully busy people. They are constantly on deadline, and therefore don't want to get inundated with emails. As a result, reporters sometimes make it a little difficult to connect with them for pitches.

So how does one get media contact information?

Well, the best approach is to subscribe to a professional database like Cision. With Cision, reporters' information is regularly updated, and there also is the ability to distribute media materials directly to reporters through the database.

Here are some options if you do not have access to Cision:

1. **Media outlet websites.** If you know the media outlet that you want to reach, check out its website. Often there will be a "Contact Us" or "Staff Directory" page. While these pages may not be highly prominent on the site, you can use Google for a site search. For instance, here's how I find the staff directory for the StarTribune using Google: **"Staff Directory" site:www.startribune.com**

2. **Twitter.** There are many lists on the internet of journalists who are on Twitter. Start following the journalists that are of interest to you; if they happen to follow you back, then you can send them a direct message.
3. **Help a Reporter Out (HARO).** With HARO, journalists post their queries -- the news stories for which they need sources. By taking a look at these queries, you will be able to get a sense of which reporters are covering the stories in your key topic areas.
4. **Bylines.** Many reporters have their email address or other contact information next to their byline or the end of the article; some TV reporters have their email address under their name on the screen.

So, in essence, if you do not have Cision, one of the best ways to get in touch with reporters is to be "media aware." This involves keeping your eyes peeled and ears tuned in for reporters that might be interested in your story. Developing relationships with those reporters will help them to be more receptive to your pitch.

Finally, you could always contact the main number for the media outlet and go through the operator; it's easier when you have the direct line to a reporter, though.

UNDERSTANDING MEDIA LEAD TIMES

With our in-the-now mentality, it can be difficult to think a season ahead. But that's exactly what's necessary to successfully pitch media outlets with long lead times.

Lead times vary with how frequently a media outlet publishes an issue or runs a particular segment. Here's a quick guide:

- **Magazines:** Lead times are most important to consider when pitching magazines. Depending on the publication, lead times can vary from two to five months or more. If you're unsure about which issue the editorial staff is currently working on, feel free to contact them. They will provide you insight into how far ahead you should be in touch.
- **TV and Radio:** In general, broadcast outlets plan their coverage first thing every morning as well as provide updates throughout the day. After all, who knows when a fire or some other breaking news event is going to happen? If you're pitching an event, it works out best to send a media advisory a couple of weeks before the event and then again the day before the event. That way the media outlet at least will have the information to consider for coverage.

- **Newspapers:** Slightly similar to TV and radio, newspapers cover the news of the day. For regular features like business briefs, event calendars, etc., expect your item to take a few weeks to run. The best approach is to look at the particular section you want to pitch and see if there is information about how far in advance information needs to be sent for publication.

With some planning, you can successfully get your information into the media's hands at the right time.

WHERE TO SEND PRESS RELEASES

At some point in the press release development process, you'll want to think about where to send press releases. After all, you want to ensure that your press release lands in the hands of the appropriate media contacts who can help you communicate with your target audience.

So what's the best way to do that? Typically, the answer is a combination of direct contact by email with broader outreach via news wire service.

To connect with reporters by email, obviously you'll need their email addresses. If you don't subscribe to a media contact database such as Cision, keep a keen eye out for media contact information in places such as at the end of stories, as graphics during TV segments, or on a magazine masthead.

Some best practices to consider when contacting the media by email include:

- Use a third-party email service provider such as MailChimp, which provides the recipients an opportunity to unsubscribe if desired. (Cision also has email distribution with this capability.)

- If using your own email client (e.g., Microsoft Outlook, Gmail):
  - Paste the text of your press release in the email, rather than sending an attachment. This saves the media contact a step. In addition, some reporters are wary of opening attachments for fear of viruses.
  - Send one email per person.
  - If you feel the need to send one email to many recipients, use the bcc field and limit each email to no more than 20 recipients.

In some instances, there are specific email addresses for unique features (such as SmallBizCal@startribune.com for the Minneapolis Star Tribune "On the Docket" business event listing). In other instances, you would visit a specific webpage (such as to submit material for paid placements such as the Minneapolis/St. Paul Business Journal's "People on the Move" and "Companies on the Move").

Think about your target audience. Do they live in a specific geographic area? Do they work in a certain industry? This will help you to know which radio programs they listen to, which blogs they read, and more.

If your service or product could appeal to anyone across the U.S. or in other countries, you would want to consider augmenting your direct media contact with a press release distribution via a wire service (e.g., Business Wire, PR Newswire, PRWeb). This also provides your organization's employees and supporters with an easy way to access and share the news, and could help your website with search engine optimization.

Of course, sending your press release via email and a wire service doesn't guarantee that your desired media contacts will see your news and act upon it. That's why follow-up phone calls are important.

DETERMINING PRESS RELEASE DISTRIBUTION

So let's say that you have written a press release or media advisory and know the reporters or media outlets that you want to reach. What is the best way to send them the material? Well, it depends.

If you work for, or your client is, a publicly-held company, then the press release should go out on a wire service such as Business Wire or PR Newswire to satisfy disclosure requirements. I have generally found, though, that reporters are not able to capture all of the information that goes out on the wires and might not see your news.

Therefore, it helps to supplement the wire distribution with direct reporter contact. This involves sending the material to the reporter in whatever way he or she chooses to receive it (email, fax, mail). Those preferences for receiving information can be found in a media database such as Cision or Vocus. Another powerful feature of media databases is the ability to send individual emails to contacts in a media list. Otherwise, you can just use your regular email program to reach out to reporters.

Given that reporters have busy schedules, it also helps to follow up your press release distribution with a phone call. This call should be a brief, 30-second pitch about why the story would be of interest to the media outlet's readers or viewers.

DON'T STOP USING THE PHONE: THE IMPORTANCE OF FOLLOW-UP CALLS

The art of the media pitch is a difficult skill to master. Media pitching begins with a newsworthy story, customized media list and typically, a specially crafted email. After delivering what you think is a brilliant, personalized pitch, reporters may take hold to the idea or may not even respond.

The question of following up after a lack of response is debated by many PR pros. Reporters and journalists, in most cases, do not have time to respond if they are uninterested or if the pitch came at the wrong time.

So why make these follow-up calls?

The laundry machine effect

We all know that when a pair of socks is washed, one mysteriously disappears. In similar fashion, emails can often fall through the cracks. Journalists and reporters can receive hundreds or thousands of emails per day. If they didn't respond, don't assume they aren't interested. Refresh their memory in an engaging way.

A second chance

A follow-up call allows you to reframe your pitch. If they didn't respond well to the original pitch, change your angle and try to reframe your pitch in a different or more newsworthy way. Do your research on each journalist and tailor your story according to his or her particular beat or content produced on the media outlet.

Beats change

Journalists often switch beats and cover a variety of topics. You may have caught a reporter at a time when they are not be interested, but know a colleague who would. Make the call to reach the right contact.

Build relationships

It's much more memorable to hear a name over the phone than reading it over email. Using follow-up calls can not only secure placements for your clients but can help create a relationship between contacts you only slightly know or still have yet to connect with.

PREPARING FOR A NEWSPAPER OR MAGAZINE INTERVIEW

Preparation can be the key to success if you're going to be interviewed by a newspaper or magazine reporter. Considering time constraints and efficiency, you probably will be interviewed over the phone.

So to get ready, here are some suggestions.

Start out by gathering some background information on the reporter and the publication. By doing research on the types of stories that the reporter has written as well as his or her educational and professional background, you can get a perspective on the types of questions that the reporter might ask in the interview.

As in any type of interview, think of two or three messages or key points that you want to communicate. In the ideal situation, one of these key messages would be the headline or the news hook of the story. If you know what you want to get out of the interview, you will be able to stay focused and bring the interview back on track if you see it going off course.

Print (newspaper or magazine) interviews differ from

television or radio ones in a couple of ways, according to media trainer Mary Milla:

- Newspaper quotes run about 10 to 25 words. To avoid getting misquoted, keep your answers to fewer than 75 words.
- Print reporters can conduct longer interviews and have more research time.
- If there's something that you don't know the answer to, you can say "I don't know," and get back to the reporter.

As in any interview, avoid "no comment," because it leaves a guilty impression. Remember that you're always on the record; if you don't want something in the story, don't say it.

Finally, if a reporter calls you and wants to interview you right away, it's OK to ask what his or her deadline is, what types of questions he or she has, and to tell him or her that you will call him or her back.

TV INTERVIEW TIPS

Your public relations professional just scored a TV interview for you – congratulations! Now what?

Let's take a look at how you can shine and represent your organization effectively.

First, get some background information on the reporter or the TV show. Look at some previous interviews – is the reporter generally hard-hitting, or relatively neutral? It's good to have a feel for the reporter's personality.

Second, prepare by developing and practicing two or three key messages or major points. Know what you want to communicate – think of this as the headline or news hook.

According to presentation and media trainer Mary Milla of What's Your Point?, TV interviews differ from radio or newspaper interviews in a couple of key ways:

- A broadcast soundbite runs nine to 15 seconds. In order to not get misquoted, Milla recommends limiting your answers to 75 words (about 30 seconds).
- TV interviews typically are short, and the reporters are

generally not well-versed in the topic.

Finally, be energetic! In the interview, answer the reporter's questions with energy and enthusiasm. That helps you to come across as credible. (Just don't go overboard like Tom Cruise on Oprah's couch!)

Oh, and by the way, everything is on the record. Be careful with what you say; if you don't want something to be used, don't say it. And don't say "no comment" – it just leaves the impression of guilt. Good luck!

RADIO INTERVIEW TIPS

So far we've discussed preparing for TV interviews as well as for print (newspaper or magazine) interviews. Getting ready for a radio interview involves a combination of the recommended preparation for a TV or print interview.

As in any interview, it's helpful to know the background information of the radio show and the person who will be interviewing you. Does the show tend to lean toward one side or the other politically? Is the interviewer generally enthusiastic and positive or often stirring up negativity?

Also, think about your objective for the interview – what you want to get as a result of participating. Consider your key messages; you will want to often come back to these during the interview. Write down supporting facts or examples that you can use during the interview. A great aspect of radio interviews is that they are usually done over the phone; even if the interview is in the studio, you can have your notes in front of you.

According to presentation and media trainer Mary Milla of What's Your Point?, radio interviews have the following characteristics:

- They are generally short (five to 10 minutes long).
- The reporters often know a little bit about the topic.
- A broadcast soundbite typically lasts nine to 15 seconds, so limit your answers to about 30 seconds to avoid being misquoted.

As always, remember to be enthusiastic and to avoid saying "no comment."

WHAT TO DO WHEN A REPORTER CALLS

The phone rings. It's a reporter from the local television station on the line, and he wants to talk to an executive at your company right away.

What do you do? First, take a deep breath. You don't need to respond right away – start by asking the reporter some questions, such as:

- When is your deadline?
- What is the angle of your story?
- How will the interview be conducted – over the phone, in person, via satellite, etc.?
- Whom else are you interviewing for the story?

Take note of the reporter's answers. Be sure to write down all of the reporter's contact information, and then tell the reporter that you will get back to him in time for his deadline. Then connect with the appropriate subject matter expert and prepare him or her for the interview.

In terms of deadlines, they are critically important to meet – both for the reporter and for you. If you don't get back to a reporter in time, your organization or client probably will not be included in the story.

HOW TO LEVERAGE MEDIA COVERAGE

The proactive media relations process can be long yet exciting. From creating the media list to developing the pitch to placing the story, it takes a lot of effort.

Once the story runs, you need to make the most of the opportunity.

Here are some ways to leverage media coverage:

1. **Internal communications.** Your employees take pride in your organization. If you share the news story with them via company email or the intranet, they will be in the know and may share the piece with family, friends and clients.
2. **Social media.** Most media outlets today have websites. It's quite easy to share links to the story with your fans and followers on company Facebook, Twitter and other social media profiles.
3. **Direct mail.** If the piece you secured ran in a newspaper or magazine, get reprints made and send to your prospects to enhance credibility and provide another opportunity to connect.
4. **Lobby.** Whether it's the waiting area of your headquarters or in the lobby of regional sales offices, get reprints made

of print pieces for visitors to read. Air TV stories on a video monitor if you have one.
5. **Website.** Many companies have a newsroom section of their website. Media coverage is just one element of what goes in this section of your website. (For more insights regarding your online pressroom, read the "If they can find it, they will come: Optimizing your online pressroom" article.[1]

After putting in all the effort to secure a story, take it further to leverage the media coverage so it works for you.

CHURCH PUBLIC RELATIONS

Vacation Bible school. Job transition groups. Fun runs. As I look in the local Apple Valley SUNThisweek newspaper, I realize that the only stories about churches are short event listings.

As I broaden my search to include the Star Tribune, there's news of the Archdiocese of St. Paul and Minneapolis considering a $165 million capital campaign, the closing of St. John's in the Dayton's Bluff neighborhood on St. Paul's East Side, and Blaine approving the permit for a small Islamic school.

A look at the St. Paul Pioneer Press reveals stories about a unique golf event called the Tournament of the Saints, a Mormon church-owned NBC television station in Utah planning to air first-run "Saturday Night Live" episodes for the first time, and the world's only ordained Hmong Episcopal priest.

Why the shortage of church-related news stories? There are a couple of reasons.

First, news stories related to religion have to meet the same news standards that secular stories meet. Uniqueness counts. (Think about the bands that the Basilica Block Party brings in each year, or the story about local Christian rock group Go Kids Music and its first album hitting No. 2 in the iTunes children's music section.[1])

Second, churches are understaffed. At the church that I attend, I know that the pastor has so much on his plate that I wouldn't be surprised if some sermons are drafted on Sunday morning before church. How could the church staff members even find time to think about, yet implement, media outreach?

Which leads to the last point ... many people at religious institutions probably don't understand public relations or even have heard of PR. The Archdiocese of St. Paul and Minneapolis has a full-time public relations manager, so it is savvy. But for the average church down the street, there's probably an unawareness of how editors decide which stories to run.

Information about Sunday sermons or the children's Christmas program isn't going to cut it as media pitches. I know that the religious institutions in the Twin Cities are doing outstanding work in their communities, and I wish them the best of luck in getting media visibility for that work.

CHANGES AND CONSTANTS IN MEDIA RELATIONS

Despite the many changes in media relations over the past few years, there are core aspects that still are important. Writing. Knowing the intricacies of one's client or company business. Relationships.

Michael Walsh, ABC, APR, MBC, former vice president, public relations for U.S. Bank Wealth Management; Roman Blahoski, director of global communications for Ecolab; and Tammy Nienaber, former director of communications for Great Clips, shared their media relations insights at an International Association of Business Communicators — Minnesota event in 2016 hosted by Spong (now Carmichael Lynch Relate).

Blahoski shared a couple of war stories from his career. One involved when he was working at ADM and a movie was released – "The Informant!" – about an ADM employee whistle-blowing on the company's price fixing. As ADM no longer engaged in that practice, Blahoski led a media relations outreach campaign with the company offering to answer any questions related to the topic. Only one outlet took the company up on the offer, and the topic faded away as the movie fizzled.

Nienaber's war story, which she referred to as "The Gastonia Incident," was a situation in which a disgruntled Great Clips employee from Gastonia, N.C., posted a photo to Facebook of hair clippings in a dumpster, stating that's where hair donations to Great Clips go. In that instance, Great Clips replied on Facebook and kept the conversation contained.

Panelists cited social media as the biggest change in media relations. Walsh uses Twitter in particular as a way to learn more about a journalist.

"Any small thing can become a large thing in social media," said Blahoski.

Nienaber also encouraged attendees to ensure that they have a professional personal brand on social media.

With all three working in corporate environments, they also shared wisdom on managing up. For instance, Walsh offers an alternative situation to an executive when he knows a news release isn't the appropriate tactic.

Blahoski likes to turn the tables by asking, "If you didn't work at this company, how interested would you be in this information?"

Evaluation, the last step in the public relations four-step process, was covered as well. Panelists said incenting audiences to change behaviors should be the main measurement, although they also use online share of voice, impressions, number of clips and placement in specific media outlets as metrics.

Changes in public relations keep the field exciting to many. "If you're just starting out, embrace how varied PR can be," said Walsh.

PART TWO
MEDIA RELATIONS 201

HOW TO BUILD RELATIONSHIPS WITH REPORTERS

In the "old days" (up until probably the late 1970s/early 1980s), Minneapolis public relations professionals often connected with reporters at a local watering hole.

In the decades since then, both public relations professionals and reporters have become busier as their organizations have worked to trim expenses by doing more with less.

Meeting a reporter in person goes a long way in he or she being receptive to your pitch. So how does one make those connections in today's busy society? Here are some tips for building relationships with reporters.

Go to media panel events hosted by professional associations such as Minnesota PRSA or IABC Minnesota. These events provide opportunities for journalists to interact with public relations professionals on a more efficient basis.

Get to know a journalist's work. As you follow their stories, you'll get a sense of which topics would make appropriate pitches. An on-target pitch will have a better shot at a positive reception.

Follow reporters on social media. Comment on their posts. Retweet their tweets. Get to know what interests them.

Ask a reporter to coffee, as some journalists still will make time for an in-person meeting. If you do secure a coffee meeting, make the most use of the opportunity by doing research on the journalist and his or her media outlet beforehand and coming prepared with relevant story ideas. Keep in mind that some journalists may be required by their employers, due to ethical considerations, to go Dutch treat or to pick up the tab.

Read Q&As and profiles of media contacts in places including Cision, PR News and Bulldog Reporter. These pieces often provide insights into a reporter's pet peeves and favorite topics. If you pay attention to these details, things will go smoother when you reach out to a reporter.

While hanging out at the local watering hole as a way to connect with journalists has gone by the wayside, there are several other ways to build relationships with reporters today.

BEYOND THE PRESS RELEASE: DEVELOPING OTHER MEDIA MATERIALS

Since the inception of public relations, the press release has been the standard tactic to gain the attention of media. Although the press release is in no way deceased, providing other media materials in addition to the press release paints a bigger picture for reporters.

Here are eight other media materials you can develop to expand your media relations efforts:

Expert source relationship

Reporters who enterprise their own stories look for credible sources to speak on their field of expertise. Creating this relationship will not only gain exposure for you and your business, but has the potential to lead to other speaking engagements. To learn more about creating an expert source relationship, check out Page 85.

Fact sheet/backgrounder

Since press releases are usually short and succinct, fact sheets and backgrounders are a great way to provide reporters with more information. Fact sheets list the high-level details of your company and a backgrounder tells the story of your company. These two documents are often part of a media kit or online pressroom.

Fact sheets include:

- Company name
- Address and phone number
- Focus of business
- Products or services
- Executive team members

Backgrounders include:

- Brief history of the company including how and why company was started
- Products or services
- Management team and roles
- Contact information

Executive biographies

Along with fact sheets and backgrounders, executive biographies are a great tool to keep in your media kit. They build the credibility of your team and can aid in positioning your brand. Reporters often look to executive biographies when writing stories on the company as a whole or individual leaders. Include the unique talents and background of each executive in his or her biography.

Q&A with CEO

A Q&A with the CEO can provide an opportunity to humanize the company story. Certain outlets have Q&A sections that feature CEOs/executives when new businesses are created, awards are won, or new products hit the market. In addition to sending out a news release to outlets, pitching execs for Q&A articles is a great way to generate awareness and add a personal touch.

Short videos

Videos can tell stories in an engaging and creative way. They can also get a business' point across in less time than traditional methods. In our 2016 public relations trends blog post,[1] we learned that video helps brands capture the attention of viewers, thus increasing their attention span. Short videos can be used in addition to press releases, media alerts and social media posts.

Check out a few infographics from Wistia[2] to see the science behind video marketing and engagement.

Social media influence

You don't need to have a million social media followers to be an influencer.

- Curate content that both highlights your business and the industry in general.
- Network with other companies in your industry and develop relationships on the social stratosphere.
- Make people want to share your content – find creative ways to deliver the simplest messages.

Although social media has no rule, just like in every other aspect of your business, your social media needs to follow your brand standards. Keeping all social media accounts consistent in terms of message and content will help build your social brand.

Blogging

Blogging has many benefits. It generates traffic to your site, boosts your place in search and helps create an expert perspective, since it is considered a form of thought leadership. Blogs can be used as supplementary writing material, giving reporters more background information on your company or product.

Here are some ideas to get your blog rolling:

- Write about company news
- Provide insight on trends in your industry
- Address current topics in your industry
- Feature different staff members

Bylined article

As mentioned above, companies sometimes use their blogs to write on current topics in the industry. Many outlets accept similar articles, called bylined articles. These articles add an expert perspective to their publications. Bylined articles help establish credibility with a large audience and draw awareness to your business. If your article focuses on an issue on your industry, offering a solution using your expertise can help attract new clients.

Here are three steps to writing your first bylined article:

- Find an outlet that focuses on your target audience
- Pitch your byline idea
- Write your article!

Next time you are creating your public relations strategy, explore your options beyond the traditional press release. Oftentimes, adding one or two additional resources can make the difference in landing a media placement.

WHEN TO HOLD A PRESS CONFERENCE

To many company executives, their news is the biggest in the world. They want to shout the news from the rooftops with a press conference/news conference, expecting that reporters will cover the story as front page news. But to many reporters, the company news is ... boring.

So how does an organization know when to hold a press conference? The short answer is when there's enough media interest in a topic that a press conference is needed in order to efficiently disseminate the information simultaneously to media outlets.

Think about the organizations or people who regularly hold press conferences. The president. Coaches of professional sports teams. Police. Does your organization's or client's news reach that level of importance and media interest? If not, perhaps a press release will suffice.

But if your news is important enough for a press conference, here are some tips for conducting a successful press conference courtesy of Bulldog Reporter.

- Select a location that will be easy for media

- representatives to get to with minimal travel time.
- Set a day (avoid Fridays and days before holidays) and time (between midmorning and midafternoon) for the press conference.
- Distribute a media advisory in advance of the press conference to inform reporters of the event.
- Prepare the press conference spokesperson with a statement and by rehearsing the entire press conference.
- Anticipate questions and prepare appropriate answers.
- Develop a media kit to distribute at the press conference, including information such as names and titles of press conference participants, a press release, fact sheet, etc.
- Create appropriate visual materials such as photos, slides, posters or even a video.
- Arrange the room in advance. Ensure that there are enough chairs. Leave a center aisle for photographers. Be sure that the lectern can accommodate multiple microphones.

Thanks to advances in technology, another option to consider is an online news conference. With an online news conference, reporters don't have to leave their desks – and media worldwide can participate.

Whether conducting an online news conference or a traditional press conference, it is essential to ask yourself if there is enough media interest to make it worthwhile. After all, you don't want to waste the media's time – or yours.

THE VALUE OF A MAT RELEASE

A MAT release is a fast way to deliver your message to a broad audience. The term MAT comes from the 1950s, essentially meaning camera-ready. During this time, newspapers were physically laid out and formatted. Although the layout process is mostly online now, the name remained.

Today's MAT release is typically a 500 to 700-word ready-to-publish article geared toward a consumer audience. As more people are reading news online, the MAT release not only includes print newspapers but online placements on media sites as well.

Content marketing agency Brandpoint is one of the leaders in distributing MAT releases, and is located here in Minnesota. Kristi Marquardt, senior business development manager at Brandpoint, offered insight on MAT releases.

"The value of the MAT release helps complement your current marketing and public relations efforts," said Marquardt. "Brandpoint guarantees top placements such as the Los Angeles Times, Chicago Tribune, San Francisco Gate as well as second-tier placements in local markets."

Aside from appearing in top-tier publications, MAT releases have the ability to reach millions.

"The placements we receive are guaranteed 800 placements and 35 million audience reach," said Marquardt. "However, on average we see 1,000 placements and 50 million audience reach."

In order to gain attention of the millions Marquardt is referring to, it's important to tailor your content to the average reader. Some of Brandpoint's gold-standard topics are:

- Home improvement
- Real estate
- Health
- Careers
- Baby boomers
- Food
- Seasonal

Aside from a gold-standard topic or theme, other tips on successful MAT releases include:

- Catchy headline that hooks editors
- Timely theme
- Transparent copy that not only is attractive to editors, but readers as well
- Family appeal
- High-quality, eye-catching photography

With the extensive reach that a MAT release can garner, consider this tactic for your next media relations campaign.

THOUGHT LEADERSHIP VIA BYLINED ARTICLES

In a previous chapter, we mentioned widening the breadth of your public relations strategy by creating media materials beyond the press release. One of the Skogrand PR Solutions recommendations was to use bylined articles to increase media coverage. Additionally, the use of thought leadership is a growing trend for public relations, becoming an integral part of strategy.

Thought leadership involves experts tapping into their talents to generate a conversation about a problem on the minds of their target audience. Outlets often feature articles written by experts to add a skilled perspective on industry issues. These articles written by industry experts help establish credibility with a large audience and can draw awareness to your business.

So how do you go about generating thought leadership?

Find your target publication

Start by determining whom you are trying to reach. If you are interested in reaching a general audience, try searching local outlets. If you are looking for a specific industry audience, try searching for more niche publications. It's very important to consider your audience when selecting publications.

Next, do research on each potential outlet you find:

- Do they accept bylined articles?
- How have they used bylined articles before?
- Do they fit your needs?
- Whom is the appropriate contact to reach out to?

Send your pitch email/call

Craft a small elevator speech on your qualifications and ask if there are any opportunities to write a bylined article for that outlet. Send your pitch to the editor via email or call him/her over the phone. When speaking with the editor, ask about potential opportunities, policies and guidelines (e.g., word count, exclusivity) required by the publication.

Begin to write

Once you secure your placement, pick a topic that is relevant to the industry. Sometimes editors may request you to write on a specific topic but if not, try writing about a current issue or trend in the industry. Offer your perspective and suggestions regarding the issue. At this time it is OK to mention how your expertise could help someone in this situation but it's important not to overpromote.

Typically, bylined articles are written after connection with the editor is made. However, if you are familiar with the outlet and the bylined guidelines it is OK to pitch the editor on a pre-written article. Skogrand PR Solutions client Jim Zuehlke of Cardinal Board Services took the pre-written approach with his Business Forum piece on risk in the Star Tribune's Business section.

Promote your piece

After your bylined article runs, feel free to promote it with your network. Buy reprints, embed the published article on your website and promote it on LinkedIn.

OPTIMIZING YOUR ONLINE PRESSROOM

In today's busy world, having an easily accessible and organized online pressroom can make the difference as to whether your company is included in a reporter's story or not. The blurred definition of "journalist" means that, in addition to reporters from traditional media outlets, bloggers and even consumers are accessing your online pressroom for information. Saving people a phone call gives them – and you – precious time. What are the criteria for today's online pressrooms? What considerations should be taken in building or updating a website?

The pressroom in a social media world

As websites have evolved over the years, so have online pressrooms. Improvements have included easier navigation, increased ease of use and added content. In the last decade, as social media use has skyrocketed, Web 2.0 tools have crept in as well.

The most common Web 2.0 tool to be added to online pressrooms is RSS (Really Simple Syndication) feed, providing journalists with a fast and easy way to read regularly updated Web content such as press releases.

Photography and video also have become increasingly popular. For Lauren Coleman-Lochner, retail reporter for Bloomberg News Service, having company advertisements in online pressrooms has been very helpful. "I don't watch that much TV, so I don't necessarily see the ads," she says.

To benefit from your online pressroom, journalists need to be able to find it first. Terms that reporters use in search engines are as unique as snowflakes. You need to accommodate them all to make your online pressroom accessible and to escalate its online visibility. Some journalists use the term "media" or "press" and the company name; while others type in the company name and "headquarters" – still others use the name of the company with the name of the CEO or media contact.

What reporters need

Simply posting press releases is not enough these days for an online pressroom. Remember, most journalists do not rely on the company website as their main source of company news.

"We get most press releases sent to us," says Roger Buoen, managing editor for MinnPost, an online news site based in Minneapolis. "I have never used them [online pressrooms] for a press release, but rather for media contact information."

Indeed, having the names, numbers and email addresses of your company's media contacts easily available is probably the most crucial aspect of an online pressroom. After all, reporters often need to conduct interviews to complete their stories.

So, what should be included in an online pressroom? Here is a sample list:

- Press releases, including PDF versions that can be downloaded and printed

- Media contact information
- Company history
- Management roster along with respective bios
- Q&A
- Photography (various formats and sizes)
- Company statistics
- Graphs and charts
- Company timeline
- Links to financial filings
- Videos
- Logos

Of course, you could include much more depending on your company and the nature of its business.

Naturally, reporters have come across their share of bad online pressrooms. Buoen says that the bad ones make it difficult to find the press releases, media contacts, company management list and corporate address. "Where the company is located is important to stories," Buoen says, "and you would be surprised how many companies do not put their corporate address out there." Other top reporter complaints include pressrooms that are not easily accessible from the company homepage or are difficult to navigate.

An extra set of arms and legs

At its best, an online pressroom can serve as an extra media relations team member who gives reporters the information that they want when they want it.

"I really like it when I can get what I need from an online pressroom and not have to call," says Nicole Garrison, former reporter for the St. Paul Pioneer Press. Garrison estimated that (when she was a journalist; she's now in public relations) she visited online pressrooms a couple of times a week, and about half the time the pressroom provided her with what she needed without having to contact the company.

For Coleman-Lochner, online pressrooms serve as verification. In the world of Wall Street, Coleman-Lochner does not rely just on wire services to ensure that company earnings releases are legitimate. "If a company comes out with a big announcement, we won't attribute it to the company until we can confirm directly with the company by their posting on their website," she says.

In some instances, your company's online pressroom can be the deciding factor on whether your company is included in the story.

Buoen, who used to work at the Minneapolis Star Tribune, relates one example: "At the paper, we used to put together graphics about companies, such as revenue and where it is located. The easier it is to find information, the more likely a graphic will occur. If it requires a lot of phone calls, we just won't do a graphic."

If managed correctly, an online pressroom can save time for you and for the journalists who cover your organization as well as provide a boost to your company's visibility. It's important to work with your company's IT and marketing departments to ensure that your organization's pressroom isn't an afterthought.

How to make your online pressroom meet today's changing media needs

1. **Keep it simple.** Reporters are often on deadline and need information right away. Make it easy for them to find what they need.
2. **Make media contact information prominent.** Often reporters just want to pick up the phone and call

someone. They become frustrated when phone numbers are not readily available.
3. **Ensure easy access from your company's homepage.** While many departments of a company compete for precious homepage real estate, if reporters cannot find your media information then your organization may not make it into the story.
4. **Provide RSS feeds.** Rather than checking frequently to see if your company has released information, RSS feeds can give reporters your company's news as it happens.
5. **Keep your online pressroom organized.** Clutter and chaos have no place in an online pressroom.
6. **Use the terms "media" and "press" in your online pressroom.** A reporter's typical Google search to find media materials is either "media" and the company name or "press" and the company name. If you use both, reporters have a better chance of finding you.
7. **Offer a search box.** While your online pressroom should be intuitive and easy to navigate, offering a box in which reporters can search for specific terms can help them find information.
8. **Provide more than just press releases.** Online pressrooms that provide executive bios, company statistics, research, downloadable content and more give reporters story ideas as well as the information that they need.

These insights are from an article that Brant wrote with search engine optimization expert Chris Peterson for the publication TACTICS.

COMPANY NAME CHANGES

In 2012, I (Brant) wrote about an issue that my wife had with LivingSocial and a Twin Cities-based Zerona laser treatments provider named Maple Grove Wellness.

Since that post, Maple Grove Wellness changed its name to Non-Surgical Clinic of the Twin Cities. I read many other complaints online related to Zerona laser treatments and LivingSocial deals with Maple Grove Wellness, so I'm assuming that the provider changed its name to just start over with its reputation.

Sometimes that's what it takes. On a bigger scale, here's a look at some companies who changed their names presumably to avoid future controversy:

- ValuJet Airlines – This low-cost airline carrier ran into reputation problems because of emergency landings, issues with quality assurance procedures, and one of the highest accident rates in the low-fare sector. The highest-profile incident with ValuJet came on May 11, 1996, when a plane flying from Miami to Atlanta crashed in the Florida Everglades, killing all 110 people on board. ValuJet's reputation never recovered, and the airline merged with

the much smaller parent company of AirTran Airways. After the 1997 merger, the ValuJet name disappeared. AirTran Airways was acquired by Southwest Airlines in 2011.
- Philip Morris Companies Inc. – While the official reason for the name change in 2003 to Altria was to provide greater "clarity" reflecting the "evolution" of the company, the organization most likely just wanted to distance itself from publicity nightmares – such as then-company president William Campbell's 1994 sworn testimony to Congress that "I believe nicotine is not addictive."
- Blackwater – The company changed its name to Xe Services LLC in an attempt to leave behind issues from the Iraq War, such as charges related to a 2007 shooting that left 17 unarmed Iraqi civilians dead. In 2011, the company changed its name again – this time to Academi.

Some company name changes are just plain dumb, such as Netflix's abandoned plan to change the name of its DVD-by-mail service to Qwikster. Or how about when Canada's Conservative Party and Reform Party merged to form the Conservative Reform Alliance Party (C.R.A.P.)? Realizing their mistake, that name quickly was changed to Canadian Reform Conservative Alliance.

COORDINATING A SUCCESSFUL MEDIA TOUR

At one point in my public relations career, I worked for Thrivent Financial, where a key initiative that I worked on was publicizing the organization's investment expertise.

Given that it's important to meet reporters face to face whenever possible, I decided to coordinate a media tour in New York with one of our top mutual fund portfolio managers.

I wasn't quite sure where to start, though — do I book appointments first or the logistics? How long should each appointment be?

Here's how I coordinated a successful media tour, step by step.

1. **Create a target media list.** The main reason I chose New York for the media tour was that it's one of the world's top financial hubs, and as a result has a high concentration of reporters covering finance. As traffic can be very congested in New York, it's very helpful to map out exactly where your target media offices are located.
2. **Decide on dates with your subject matter expert.**

Two days in New York turned out to be appropriate. In addition to my schedule and the mutual fund portfolio manager's schedule, I looked to see if there were any big events going on in New York at that time. I wanted to be able to connect with as a many media contacts as possible.

3. **Start reaching out.** Begin with your priority media to determine their availability. Schedule half an hour for your appointments to be conscious of everyone's time, but block out an hour for each appointment in case meetings go long so you can stay on schedule. (Also, be sure to leave time for traffic jams!)
4. **Coordinate travel plans.** In addition to flights and hotels, you're going to need a way to easily get around New York. In my case, we booked with BostonCoach. That provided a car waiting for us outside of the building after each appointment.
5. **Develop briefing materials.** Reporters want to have something that they can refer to, take notes on and use in case they decide to do stories. Put the information in a folder that can left behind. Some ideas of information to include are: recent news releases, a fact sheet about your organization and subject matter expert bios.
6. **Send reminders.** As reporters have very hectic schedules, it's a smart idea to remind them a day before the media tour about the appointment.
7. **Enjoy the media tour!** It was a thrill to go from place to place and tell reporters about the excellent initiatives underway at Thrivent Financial.

While organizing the Thrivent Financial media tour took a lot of time and effort, it was worth it; the reporters whom I met with ended up doing stories on Thrivent Financial's investment offerings.

DEVELOPING AN EXPERT SOURCE RELATIONSHIP WITH THE MEDIA

Media relations has many uses, but is often used for one goal: promoting your business. One of the most economical ways to gain mass exposure is to be included in news media stories. Although your story pitches for features on your business may not be picked up by reporters, there is another way to position yourself to the media – developing an expert source relationship.

What is an expert source relationship?

In order for outlets and reporters to be legitimate and credible, they need sources on a variety of topics. In addition, when large national stories become of high interest, reporters look to local professionals for insight. Although they may have ideas of whom to contact, reporters often change beats and are receptive to new experts on topics of interest to them.

Creating this media relationship will not only gain exposure for you and your business, but also can lead to commentary at other outlets.

How do you create an expert source relationship?

- **Keep up with current trends.**
    - It's important to not only keep track of headlines in your area of expertise, but national and international headlines as well. Brainstorm how you can tailor stories to a local audience and find connections between your expertise and broader topics.
- **Introduce yourself.**
    - Whether this is in a phone call or over email, let your contacts know what you're available to speak on and why you are qualified to do so.
- **Do your homework.**
    - Research local media outlets and reporters to find out who typically writes on your area of expertise and generate a list of target contacts.
- **Keep your resume updated.**
    - Have your qualifications on hand so it is easy to address why you are a credible source. Mention previous speaking engagements and commentary you've provided as a reference for contacts.
- **Generate your own content.**
    - Whether it be on LinkedIn, your website or a blog, comment on issues and trends in your industry. Generating content can also help you become more visible when reporters search for experts in your field.

By being an expert resource for reporters and responding in time for their deadlines, you can have the beginnings of a mutually beneficial media relationship.

LANDING A MEDIA BRIEFING

In my public relations career, I (Brant) have found that meeting reporters in person helps tremendously in securing future media placements down the line.

Think about it – just like any human interaction, we are more likely to trust someone whom we have met in person compared to someone we have never met.

One public relations tactic that can help build relationships with reporters is called a media briefing. A media briefing essentially involves meeting with reporters in person, telling them about your client or organization, and asking how you can help the reporter with his or her work. While a media briefing may not result in a story immediately, it will assist reporters in becoming more familiar with your client or company and how you could fit into their future reporting.

Given that everyone has busy schedules, it may be challenging to secure a media briefing. Here are some tips on landing a media briefing.

First, see if your local chapter of Public Relations Society of America or International Association of Business Communicators has any media panel events planned. At these chapter events, there's usually a panel of three or four media contacts who talk about the best way to help them with their reporting, what trends they are seeing, and the types of stories they are looking for. Go to these events — and if you attend, introduce yourself to the panelists afterward and request an opportunity for a media briefing with an executive from your company or your client's organization.

Another tip involves if your company or client is exhibiting at an trade show. To attend trade shows, reporters have to register. The organizers of the trade show then have a list of registered media attending that can be requested by exhibitors. Ask for the list as soon as it's available. As there are many exhibitors requesting the list, you have to be quick. Once you obtain the list, contact the reporters and ask to get on their schedule of trade show appointments for a media briefing. Act fast, though — their schedules will fill up quickly!

Third, keep an eye out for new reporters in your city. In general, reporters have more time when they start a new position and are open to learning about the companies on their beat. Give them a call and offer a tour of your company or client's facility.

Finally, if your company or client has a new CEO or initiative to announce, that could be a perfect time to request a media briefing. Reporters always want to be in the know on the freshest news — it's their job!

USING RESEARCH FOR PUBLICITY'S SAKE

One tactic that can be very effective in obtaining media coverage for your company or client is conducting what's called a newsmaker survey, and then pitching the survey results to reporters for potential news stories.

To illustrate this tactic, I'll share with you a campaign that I (Brant) worked on at Thrivent Financial. Even though Thrivent Financial evolved beyond its life insurance roots to become a serious financial planning player, research by the organization revealed that members and prospects were not fully aware of its transformation. While members gave Thrivent Financial high marks for integrity, generous spirit and values, they gave the organization low scores on product performance and customer service. Using findings from our research and insights department, I managed our outside public relations firm in a multilayered campaign focused on rebranding the organization as a financial institution and providing tangible proof of Thrivent's financial expertise with a new online retirement planning tool called ThriveQ.

This integrated campaign included: distributing tool kits to 2,500 financial representatives, street teams dropping 5,000 "branded" quarters in downtown Minneapolis/St. Paul, an advertising "takeover" at the Minneapolis/St. Paul airport, working with an outside firm to conduct a "Thriving in Retirement" survey of 2,500 baby boomers, conducting deskside meetings with media in New York, distributing a matte column to media nationwide, conducting a satellite media tour and pitching reporters in six key geographic markets.

Results included: more than 160 million media impressions in media outlets including Reuters and USA Today, 1.73 million paid media impressions, post-campaign research conducted by the organization revealing Thrivent's brand equity to be at an all-time high with prospects (Those stating that it "has a solid reputation as a financial service company" doubled, while those who believed it "offers a wide range of financial products and services" tripled), more than 22 million media impressions related to ThriveQ, nearly 90,000 ThriveQ site visits, 30 percent of visitors completing the ThriveQ quiz, and of those visitors more than one-fifth registered for future ThriveQ and Thrivent correspondence.

Thrivent Financial used the research from the campaign to design new financial products and remain a source of financial stability through the Great Recession and beyond. The campaign won two PRSA Silver Anvil awards in 2008. In addition, the campaign won two Minnesota PRSA Classics awards.

Tips for promoting research

As you can see, this was quite a comprehensive campaign. Here are some insights that I learned from working on this award-winning campaign.

- **Focus on a relevant topic.** A survey on the financial aspects of retirement readiness is an appropriate topic for Thrivent Financial to share its expertise. Thrivent Financial members are known for doing good in their communities, so another newsmaker survey that the organization conducted focused on Americans' preferences relating to volunteering time versus giving money. Other brands who have successfully used newsmaker surveys to generate publicity include: American Express (small business), StubHub (live events) and eBay (gift giving).

- **Use an outside firm to conduct research.** Public relations professionals aren't pollsters. To ensure that the survey is credible, using a company that specializes in research is important. The survey experts will know what the appropriate sample size should be and the best way to administer the survey. They also will help you to interpret the survey results to discover what's newsworthy.
- **Share the survey methodology.** Reporters are going to want to know how the survey was conducted. Were people surveyed online, over the phone, in person, or some other method? How many survey respondents were there? What is the margin of error and the level of confidence?
- **Spread out the promotion.** Survey results can provide numerous news angles. At Thrivent Financial, we had an initial push that included a white paper, "Baby Boomers and Retirement: A Generation's Catch-22." There were more statistics that made excellent news hooks, though, so we issued subsequent news releases that focused on additional findings as news angles.

If you decide to conduct a newsmaker survey, do it right and you could create tremendous visibility for your organization or client.

WHAT TO DO IF 'THE LOOKOUT' SHOWS UP

One of my (Brant) favorite shows (although it only ran for one season) on TV was ABC's "The Lookout." If you're not familiar with it, ABC described "The Lookout" as "a survival guide to the modern consumer jungle, offering a mix of compelling undercover investigations and lively dispatches about how you spend your money."

When it comes to ambush journalism, some people just fail – while others make it through relatively unscathed.

One episode of "The Lookout" focused on cars impacted by Superstorm Sandy that were subsequently sold without flood titles.

Anyone who saw that episode probably isn't going to buy a car from D&D Auto Sales in Old Bridge, N.J.

On the other hand, after an impressive interview with Kevin J. Bergner of USAA in the same episode, one got the impression that the organization wants to do right by its members. USAA's reputation is probably intact.

It reminds me of the clip from Michael Moore's "The Big One" that featured Phil Knight, the co-founder of Nike.

What made USAA and Nike successful in those interviews? For starters, they met with the interviewers. TV can be really sensational when people are running away from the camera. Both Bergner and Knight took the time to share their positions.

Second, if something wasn't right, they offered to look into it. In USAA's case, Bergner said that it was "unsatisfactory" that vehicles were sold through USAA without the appropriate branded flood titles.

Third, they followed through. Nike did look into the minimum age issue of its Indonesian workers and eventually raised the minimum age to 18. I'm guessing that USAA followed through as well because it has a strong reputation to uphold.

Finally, the organizations made their highest-ranking person available. Bergner is the president of USAA Property and Casualty Insurance Group, and Knight is the co-founder and chairman of Nike.

THE ART OF THE APOLOGY

Authentically saying "I'm sorry" can be a very challenging action to take.

In 2014, however, Jonah Hill delivered an excellent apology on "The Tonight Show." While Hill was on the show to plug his new "22 Jump Street" movie, he insisted on clearing the air first regarding the circumstances in which he was caught on video using a gay slur directed at a paparazzo.

Hugh Grant also delivered a skillful apology on "The Tonight Show" in 1995 for his dalliance with a prostitute. Grant effectively summed it up by saying, "I did a bad thing, and there you have it."

Finally, David Letterman was deft in his apologies related to having sexual liaisons with female staff members.

How come these three apologies worked? They were sincere. They were timely. Above all, they essentially said, "I screwed up and I'm sorry."

EFFECTIVE CRISIS COMMUNICATION

A crisis, or a "people-stopping, showstopping event that creates victims" according to crisis communications expert Jim Lukaszewski, ABC, APR, Fellow PRSA, can create major havoc for an organization. One aspect particularly known to cause hand-wringing for CEOs is the negative media coverage that usually accompanies a crisis.

Lukaszewski, however, never worries about the media in a crisis; he instead focuses on the organization's behavior as the perpetrator.

At a session that I (Brant) attended led by Lukaszewski, he outlined his five-step process for effective crisis communication.

1. **Stop the production of victims.** Deal with the underlying problem first and address key issues.
2. **Manage the victim dimension.** Victims can be people, animals or living systems. Anticipate the dynamics of the victims of the crisis.
3. **Communicate with those people who need to know now.** As everyone affected becomes a communicator, it's important to inform and educate them — particularly employees.

4. **Inform the indirectly affected.** This includes people who now have a problem because the organization has a problem, such as interest groups or allies.
5. **Deal with the self-anointed and self-appointed.** In today's media environment, everyone can be a reporter – from a blogger to a journalist to someone with a Facebook account.

Lukaszewski added two core crisis communications best practices that all of us learned in kindergarten – tell the truth and apologize.

"If you take the path of truth, you get to sleep at night," said Lukaszewski. He also said that numerous times he has noticed that the negative aspects of a crisis often stop happening when the organization authentically apologizes.

Above all, remember what matters in a crisis – the victims.

WHAT DOES A PR PROFESSIONAL DO?

A common question I (Aliki) receive from family, friends or potential clients is, "What does a PR professional do?" It's one I've found difficult to answer but necessary for others to understand.

The difficulty of this question comes from the many hats a PR professional wears. Responsibilities and tactics vary by industry and individual organization, but there are core responsibilities essential to each PR professional.

To start, public relations professionals work to gain free publicity for their client and to maintain positive relationships between an organization and its publics.

So, what goes into all of that?

Writing

Public relations stems from strategic communication. Aside from verbal communication, PR is heavily reliant on strategic writing. This means writing well in order to generate exposure with a particular audience. PR professionals often write press releases, media advisories, briefing sheets, blog posts, emails and speeches.

Listening

While PR professionals create high volumes of content, listening is a necessary skill.

- What does your client want?
- What does your client need?
- What are people saying about your client?
- What is the industry saying?

By listening, content is generated to please both the client and its publics.

Storytelling

The difference between PR and advertising is that in PR exposure is free. It's important to highlight an organization in a way that will gain media attention but maintain brand identity and key messages.

Acting and reacting

In public relations, it's impossible to predict each negative event. With a proactive strategy you can foresee some negative events and plan accordingly. It is equally important to create a reactive strategy after a negative event to minimize brand damage.

WHEN TO HIRE A PR FIRM

Numerous times I (Brant) have been contacted by businesses who want to work with Skogrand PR Solutions to promote the fact that they are celebrating an anniversary. While an anniversary can be an occasion to obtain media coverage based on what your company has accomplished and to promote your vision of the organization's future, there are many other times when to hire a PR firm.

Perhaps you are able to do public relations on your own (if so, use the insights in this book). However, hiring a PR firm will help you achieve visibility while letting you focus on your business operations.

Here are some tips to help you understand when to hire a PR firm.

- **Is your company launching a new product?** A tremendous amount of energy goes into bringing a new product to market. Launching a new product could be an excellent opportunity for media coverage, and you'll want to connect with potential buyers of your new product.
- **Is an acquisition taking place?** Whether your

company is the acquirer or the one being acquired, an acquisition is newsworthy – particularly if one or both of the companies is publicly traded.
- **Is your company embarking on major expansion?** Tapping into new markets (geographic, demographic, etc.) is very exciting, and a PR firm can assist you in promoting your expansion.
- **Is your organization downsizing?** On the flip side, a PR firm can help you manage the media coverage if your company is shrinking, like the shutdown of Toys "R" Us in 2018.
- **Is there new leadership?** A PR firm can help your new CEO share his or her vision for the organization.

For more insights on if your organization's initiatives are worth promoting, read the chapter on what makes something newsworthy.

Now that you understand when to hire a PR firm, here are some things to look for in a PR firm. Search for a PR firm with experience in numerous industries. That shows they should be able to get up to speed quickly on your organization. Also, look for testimonials. Who are some of the clients the PR firm has worked with? What do they say about the firm? See if people from the PR firm are Accredited in Public Relations, which means they are committed to the best practices and highest standards of ethics of the profession.

Besides Skogrand PR Solutions, you can find other PR firms by using "Find a PR Firm" tools on the Minnesota PRSA or PRSA national websites.

HOW TO FIND A PUBLIC RELATIONS FIRM

So your organization has decided that it needs some visibility, and you have been given the task of finding a public relations firm. How do you go about finding a public relations agency? Here are some tips:

- **Start with Google.** By doing a quick Google search, you will be able to get an overview of public relations companies in your area. Use common search terms such as "public relations firms," "public relations companies," "public relations agencies," "agency public relations" and "companies public relations" to get a good snapshot.
- **Ask for referrals.** Perhaps you have friends that work for other companies who have used a public relations firm. Ask their opinion of practitioners that they have worked with, including the scope of the project, areas of expertise, cost and other questions that you might have.
- **Consult the Public Relations Society of America (PRSA).** On the PRSA website, there is a "Find a Firm" tool. It provides the opportunity to find public relations firms by name, geographic region, industry or practice specialization, and whether or not the firm

has accredited members.
- **Visit a local blog.** In Minnesota, we have the Minnesota Public Relations Blog, which includes a list of Minnesota PR agencies as well as some agency profiles.
- **Read local business publications.** In the Minneapolis-St. Paul area, Twin Cities Business provides a list of the top 25 public relations firms, and the Minneapolis/St. Paul Business Journal offers its Book of Lists for sale.

After you identify some possible firms, give them a call to describe what you're looking for and, if it seems appropriate, meet with them in person about next steps.

MEASURING MEDIA RELATIONS SUCCESS

As measuring media relations isn't an exact science, communicators often have debated appropriate metrics. Some don't quite cut it, such as advertising equivalency and the use of multipliers. So in 2010, communication leaders from the International Association for the Measurement and Evaluation of Communication (AMEC) met in Barcelona to agree upon an overarching framework for effective public relations and communication measurement. The result? The Barcelona Declaration of Measurement Principles.

In 2015, AMEC leaders convened once again to update the Barcelona Principles from focusing on "what not to do" to guidance on "what to do."

Here's a look at the updated 2015 Barcelona Principles.

- **Principle 1: Goal Setting and Measurement are Fundamental to Communication and Public Relations.** "The updated Principles recognize that they can be applied to the larger communication function of any organization, government, company or brand globally. In fact, measurement, evaluation and goal-setting should be holistic across media and paid,

earned, owned and shared channels."
- **Principle 2: Measuring Communication Outcomes is Recommended Versus Only Measuring Outputs.** "The use of qualitative methods (along with quantitative) should be used as appropriate. Advocacy (also) is an outcome that can (and should) be measured."
- **Principle 3: The Effect on Organizational Performance Can and Should Be Measured Where Possible.** "Communications impact more than just business results; rather communications can impact the overall performance of an organization. To do this, organizations must have, and practitioners must understand, integrated marketing and communication models. The PR channel does not exist in a silo, nor should PR measures."
- **Principle 4: Measurement and Evaluation Require Both Qualitative and Quantitative Methods.** "Qualitative measures are often needed in order to explain 'the why' behind the quantitative outcomes. In addition (practitioners) need focus on measuring performance (be it positive, negative or neutral), and avoid making assumptions that results will always be positive or 'successful.'"
- **Principle 5: AVEs are not the Value of Communications.** "Advertising Value Equivalents (AVEs) measure the cost of media space or time and do not measure the value of PR or communication, media content, earned media, etc."
- **Principle 6: Social Media Can and Should be Measured Consistently with Other Media Channels.** "Social media measurement tools have evolved to a point where there is greater potential for consistent measurement on engagement, along with quantity and quality."
- **Principle 7: Measurement and Evaluation Should be Transparent, Consistent and Valid.** "(An effort should

be made) to ensure quantitative methods are reliable and replicable and qualitative methods are trustworthy."

As you undertake setting goals for your next media relations of communications campaign, remember to incorporate the Barcelona Principles.

PART THREE
LET'S HEAR FROM THE JOURNALISTS AND INFLUENCERS

TWIN CITIES JOURNALISTS ADDRESS CHANGING LANDSCAPE

Journalists in Minneapolis/St. Paul are in the midst of a "new paradigm for news generation," and a few of them shared at a 2014 "Meet the Media" panel what that means for public relations professionals.

The event, sponsored by the Minnesota chapter of Public Relations Society of America, Business Wire and the Twin Cities chapter of National Investor Relations Institute, included:

- Dave Schwartz, sports reporter at KARE 11,
- Jim Hammerand, digital editor at the Minneapolis/St. Paul Business Journal,
- Julio Ojeda-Zapata, technology writer at the St. Paul Pioneer Press,
- Andy Putz, executive editor of MinnPost,
- Duchesne Drew, managing editor for operations at the Star Tribune, and
- Nancy Lebens, editor for MPR News.

According to panelists, social media, ever-tightening deadlines and media outlet collaboration are among the factors driving the changes.

For instance, Ojeda-Zapata recently was given access to the paper's content management system. "That would have been unheard of before," he said.

As could be expected, the digital aspect of media outlets is taking on increasing importance. Lebens shared that half of MPR News' website traffic comes from mobile devices. Since switching to a digital-first strategy, the Minneapolis/St. Paul Business Journal audience has grown to 400,000.

Social media is an important tool to journalists in news gathering and keeping a pulse on possible stories.

"I use Twitter the way that people used to use a scanner," said Lebens.

Ojeda-Zapata used to frequently use Google+, and his blog provides an opportunity for content that doesn't make the print edition of the paper.

To assist journalists in meeting their tight deadlines, panelists recommended that organizations have excellent newsrooms on their websites that make information easy for journalists to access. (NOTE: Check out the "Optimizing Your Online Pressroom" chapter for information on specifically what should be in an online pressroom.)

Panelists also shared some examples of the increasing collaboration of media outlets:

- KARE-TV works with MPR News to share stories.
- The Minneapolis/St. Paul Business Journal cooperates with KMSP-TV and WCCO Radio.
- In 2014 the Star Tribune started printing the St. Paul

Pioneer Press.
- Twin Cities TV stations use an overnight "pool shooter" that films breaking stories, and all stations share the resulting footage.

With all the changes, however, some aspects of collaborating with journalists are staying the same. Email is still the best way to connect. Relationships matter. Follow-up phone calls are OK. Some journalists are even up for informational coffees if their schedule allows.

WHY INFLUENCER MARKETING IS IMPORTANT

Mommy bloggers, Instagram "models," beauty gurus, the list goes on. You've seen social media users amass large followings, some in the millions. People have been chronicling their life in blog form for years out of fun or stress relief but it was only fairly recently these bloggers began to understand how to monetize their blogs by featuring products from fashion to home furnishings.

Now, more than ever, brands have begun to understand the importance of these social leaders. In fact, Tomoson[1] reports influencer marketing as the fastest-growing online customer acquisition tactic, beating out organic, paid search and email marketing. It's clear that consumers look to "thought leaders" to influence their purchasing decisions.

Why is influencer marketing growing? Simply put, there are massive amounts of social media users ... and brands are always looking for the best ways to engage with these users. According to Pew Research Center,[2] nearly-two thirds of all American adults are on social media sites and 90 percent of young adults actively participate on social sites. What does this mean? People are heavily consuming social content and it's become a part of their daily lives.

Furthermore, social media is revolutionizing the concept of word-of-mouth referrals. People always have talked about their experiences, events and products they love with friends and loved ones over lunch, drinks or the phone. With the increase of social media, people are now sharing these same experiences online. According to Nielsen,[3] 92 percent of consumers trust recommendations from others — even people they don't know. This makes word-of-mouth marketing highly effective.

Read on to learn which brands are using influencer marketing well and tips for how you can integrate this into your strategy.

INFLUENCER MARKETING BEST PRACTICES

More than ever audiences are skeptical of branded content. In the U.S., only 48% of the population trust businesses,[1] putting pressure on brands to deliver authentic content with messages consumers can believe. Consumers instead are putting their trust in someone else – influencers.

Ninety-two percent of consumers trust recommendations from other people – even someone they don't know – over brand content,[2,3] including social media influencers.

Influencers are generally people with a large online and social media following in a particular niche. These online personalities share their lives online and interact with their audience, creating a relationship to build credibility and trust.

In turn, influencers have the power to affect purchasing decisions of their followers, sharing what stores they've been shopping at for clothes, which furniture manufacturer they chose when redoing their living room, what car they recommend purchasing and more. Consumers consume the most content when it feels genuine and helpful.

Companies have pivoted with this change and begun to partner with influencers to meet business objectives and it's working; some businesses have reported up to $18 in earned media value for every dollar they spend on influencer marketing. Oftentimes, influencer marketing is less expensive than traditional advertising and reaches a more targeted audience. Overall, the influencer marketing space is expected to reach $10 billion by 2022, up from $2 billion in 2017.[4]

Additionally, influencer partnerships can help businesses:
- Grow brand awareness
- Engage with target audiences
- Increase SEO and drive referral traffic
- Secure editorial coverage
- Present product organically through third-party channels
- Elevate broader marketing initiatives
- Garner a broad range of applicable assets
- Drive sales

When partnering with influencers it's important to make strategic collaborations with defined goals. Here are a few tips:
- Define your goal upfront and pick partners that will help reach it (engagement, reach, relevance).
- It's not all about the top 100. Microinfluencers often have some of the highest engagement rates.
- Quality over quantity. It's best to have focused partnerships with the right people as opposed to many not driving the results you want.
- Build authentic relationships that last beyond one partnership.
- Provide key messages and set deliverable expectations up front.

- Measure, report, track key learnings for future partnerships and request analytics from the influencers you partner with.

As you look to expand your marketing efforts, think about including influencers into your business plans to help build your customer base and relationships with your target audiences.

BRANDS THAT HAVE SUCCEEDED WITH INFLUENCER MARKETING

Here are five brands that have found success with influencers:

Kate Spade

Kate Spade took to Pinterest influencers for its campaign.[1] The chosen influencers were instructed to put together a board with the theme "Saturday Is." They not only generated beautiful content and color inspiration for the designer, but they reached 1.2 million followers collectively.

Downy

Downy took a creative approach for its campaign.[2] The brand used soft, fabric-like sculptures to capture everyday situations. They brought influencers in by using the hashtag #SoftSide to talk about what the brand meant to them. The campaign resulted in a five-point increase in brand favorability and social media engagement doubled.

Gap

Gap[3] wanted to take the concept of a fashion blog that lives on the company site. Gap created Styld.by, a website full of outfits and inspiration created by influencers. These influencers were not limited to bloggers and social media users with large followings. The reason why the site was so successful was due to the highly interactive and authentic feeling of the posts.

Boxed Water

In Boxed Water's campaign,[4] the brand combined social cause and influencer marketing. As an effort to reduce its carbon footprint, for every Instagram post that promoted Boxed Water with the hashtag #ReTree, the organization promised to plant two trees in national forests. Boxed Water partnered with social influencers to spread the word. Nearly 74,000 trees were planted as a result of the campaign.

Johnnie Walker

Johnnie Walker wanted to capitalize on the concept of having experiences and enjoying life in the present. The Instagram strategy involved partnering with influencers with a "sense of adventure." Selected influencers traveled to Milan, Scotland and Shanghai and took pictures related to the brand to share on social. The Johnnie Walker Instagram account gained 2,000 fans in the first two weeks.

Conducting an influencer marketing campaign can feel daunting if you've never done it before. Here are tips to get the ball rolling on your next influencer marketing strategy.

1. **Do your research**
   It's important to find the influencer that will best connect you with your target audience. Oftentimes, this may not be the account with the highest amount of followers. Take the time to understand the influencers you align with best, as well as their following. The thought that goes into selecting influencers should be comparable to that of a specially-crafted media list.
2. **Personalize your outreach**
   Oftentimes influencers get many requests for marketing partnerships. The more you personalize your pitch, the more authentic you come across. It's important in these situations to build relationships and rapport to further enhance your partnership.
3. **Understand the work influencers put in**
   Whether the influencers you are working with are bloggers, vloggers or have a large audience on social media, respect the amount of work that goes into their posts. Oftentimes influencers spend hours reviewing your product and compiling a thoughtful reflection. Understand that quality may take time.
4. **Be flexible/Work together**
   Influencers know their audience the best. Allow them to offer up ideas or help collaborate. Sponsorships often sound the most authentic when the influencer is using his or her own tone and voice. Give the influencers your expectations but continue to allow them to make your campaign their own.
5. **Follow up**
   Thank them for their work and maintain a relationship in case future opportunities arise.

MEET AN INFLUENCER: BRUNO BORNSZTEIN OF CURBLY, MANMADEDIY AND INFLUENCEKIT

1. Describe the type of content that runs on your websites, Curbly.com and ManMadeDIY.com.

Curbly is a DIY, design and home improvement blog. Our goal is to help people love where they live.

ManMadeDIY is a men's lifestyle blog with a focus on craft - things like woodworking, food, outdoor activities, and tools.

2. How can a brand work with you to be included on one of your sites?

We receive a lot of unsolicited PR pitches (press releases, etc.), most of which never get on our radar. A blanket press release is not a good way to get our attention. Engaging with us on social media works much better, as does a personalized e-mail. And of course, we're happy to discuss sponsored content opportunities whenever there's a good fit.

3. Could you provide an overview of what influencer marketing is and how brands can get started with it?

Influencer marketing is, first and foremost, about brand building. It's not direct marketing, it's not affiliate marketing, and it's not about selling X number of your product. Influencer marketing is about helping you establish your brand and communicate your product's value proposition to an engaged and receptive audience. You can (and should) do this via your own content channels as well, but partnering with an influencer lends more credibility and authenticity to your message.

To get started, you need to know who's creating the best content in your niche. Influencers are not just people with a big following. Real influencers are exceptional content creators; they're the ones generating the fuel that drives the internet: amazing content! Fortunately, finding them is pretty easy: do some web searches on key terms related to your product, search social media, or just ask your customers. If all that fails, there are plenty of tools out there to help you locate influencers; if you use them, just exercise caution – they'll often cast a very wide net.

4. Share with us an overview of your new business, InfluenceKit.

InfluenceKit helps influencers prove their value and make more money with clear, automating reporting for all their sponsored content. We also help brands understand the value of their influencer marketing campaigns.

5. What are the similarities and differences between media relations and influencer marketing?

The most obvious one: money. The less obvious one: scale.

Influencers are (usually) tiny media companies. As such, they need to get paid! And sponsored content (a.k.a. influencer marketing) can represent a big portion of their revenue. So it is crucial to find a balance between monetary compensation, in-kind compensation, and organic content with an authentic voice. The best way to do this is to develop a good relationship between the sponsor and the influencer. Clear expectations, accurate reporting (hint: InfluenceKit!), and long-term (not short-term or one-off) campaigns are the best way to do that.

Scale presents a challenge because brands and agencies may have to coordinate campaigns with dozens of individual influencers. That's a lot of contracts, invoices, work briefs, and reports to wrangle. I recommend starting small and experimenting until you find a group of influencers you can really trust and rely on.

6. How do brands know that their influencer marketing investment was worth it?

Start by knowing your objectives! Then do your best to measure performance. I'm shocked how many influencers don't offer reporting by default, and even more shocked by how many brands and agencies don't ask for it! Reports help you quantify how effective an influencer marketing campaign was; how many people it reached, and how many of those people engaged with it in some way.

Caveat! Reporting is important, but it's not everything! Influencer marketing is quantitative, yes, but also qualitative. Did the campaign produce beautiful, useful content that you can reuse on your own channels? Did it give you insight into how customers view your brand? Did it give you ideas for new ways to talk about your product in the future? There are lots of benefits that are hard to quantify, but don't ignore them!

7. What are some of the most successful influencer marketing campaigns in your opinion?

I think influencer marketing is a success when you have evidence that a lot of people saw and engaged with your message on multiple platforms. I like to see campaigns where there was a diversity of content across channels (i.e. a strong blog post that can have lasting value, social media components that reached a large audience, and video/image assets that the brand can leverage).

8. Share an example of where influencer marketing went wrong.

Influencer marketing doesn't always work! I know, it's crazy, right? But just like any other marketing channel, you have to be prepared to endure some missteps along the way. I find the biggest predictor of a campaign that isn't going to succeed is when the brand wants to micromanage the direction of the content. Influencers need freedom to create content in a way they know will resonate with their audience. Another bad sign is one-off campaigns with very fast turnaround. Great content takes time and planning to execute.

9. Where do you see influencer marketing headed?

I think it's going to continue to grow, because it's actually a very effective marketing strategy. At the same time, there's a lot of hype in the market right now, so I expect a bit of backlash as well. In particular, I think we'll see a lot of so-called 'influencers' getting cut out of the equation. These days it doesn't take a lot to call yourself an 'influencer,' even if you aren't really great at creating content, and don't really have a lot of influence. Brands are getting more sophisticated, and I hope this means they'll be investing even more into working with real influencers who they can trust to create valuable content that performs.

MEET THE MEDIA: BILL SHERCK OF 'DUE NORTH OUTDOORS'

Authors' note: This Q&A originally appeared on the Skogrand PR Solutions Blog in 2014. Sherck now co-hosts "Minnesota Bound," although he still contributes to "Due North Outdoors."

Those who love the outdoors probably would consider Bill Sherck's job the position of their dreams. Sherck, known as "The Man About The Woods," can be seen on some of the country's most popular outdoor television programs, including: "Backroads with Ron & Raven" on The Versus Network, "Legends of Rod and Reel" and "Pheasants Forever Television" on the Outdoor Channel, "Minnesota Bound" on NBC in Minnesota and "Due North Outdoors," which Bill co-hosts on Fox Sports Network (North & Wisconsin).

1. Could you recap your television career before moving to outdoor television?

I actually started in college in Green Bay in the winter of 1993/spring of 1994. I had an internship at WLUK, which was an NBC affiliate. I was told that I was going to wash news vehicles and file papers. I told the person who hired me that I wanted to hang out with a team. Every night I hung out with the 10 p.m. team. I got to do some stories and build my skills.

My first full-time job was at WDIO in Duluth after graduation. Then I spent three years at the ABC affiliate in Madison, Wisconsin. My big break came when Fox News called. I got to work at an owned-and-operated station in North Carolina. I was based in High Point with a station called WGHP. It was fun because I covered local news, but then when national stories broke, I would do coverage for Fox stations around the country.

At one point, when I was covering Y2K stories in North Carolina, I started thinking about where I was in life, and decided that I wanted to come back to Minnesota. I came back to Minneapolis in 2000. I started working for Channel 5, where I spent three years.

2. How does the "Minnesota Bound" and "Due North Outdoors" team decide which places to visit and stories to cover?

I have file cabinets full of story ideas. We have far more stories than time. For "Minnesota Bound" and "Due North Outdoors," we sit around four times per year to discuss story ideas and what we have time to get done.

We work with our clients too to determine stories. Ontario Tourism is a big client, so we figure out stories with them, for example.

3. How would you describe your approach to TV storytelling?

It's storytelling ... the good, the bad, the ugly, the honest. We really don't try to make it up. We just go and document and show what we've got. Sometimes you just go out the door and things go to pot. The fish aren't biting, the big one gets away, the vehicle breaks down. That makes for the best television, though. Being honest and showing it like it is – that's what I like to do. Sometimes the stories are really great, and sometimes you get your tail handed to you. In some ways that connects with audiences better. It's television storytelling – matching words with picture and sounds, and weaving all that together.

4. What has been the most surprising or unique story that you have covered?

There are too many to list – literally thousands of stories. Doing outdoor stuff, it's amazing how many people break down, people who get emotional in our stories. Grouse hunters, for example. They break down or get emotional. People in the outdoor world are very sentimental about the places that they go. The gear means a lot to them. It's more than gear to the owner – it's how they do their sport or hobby. So many of the stories that we do, people get emotional. I understand that, because I have that kind of passion for the outdoors. It's fun to see others get so emotional.

5. You turned your focus to outdoor television in 2002. How has that type of TV changed during your career?

When I started, outdoor television was still gearing up. Many networks had more airtime than they had shows. It was very easy for us to get shows on networks. If you had high-quality stuff, it stood out. Now there's a lot more competition. Prices for camera gear have dropped also. Now you could buy a full HD camera for $4,000 to $5,000, which is significantly less than before. It allowed a lot more people to enter the arena. It improved the quality of outdoor television shows as a whole, created a lot more competition, and created competition in sales. It's a lot more difficult to get advertisers. Content in this business is secondary to sales.

Television news is still a really big deal. They have gotten away from reporting the news, though. Now they worry more about what color their tie and dress are, what kind of technology they can use and what the studio looks like.

I dealt with Magid (Frank N. Magid Associates, Inc.) in Madison, Minneapolis and Duluth. He caused me a lot of headaches over the years. Magid would come into stations and say, "TV news should look like this," and the station would change.

I never had an agent. Maybe it held me back professionally, maybe not. Andy Rooney and Walter Cronkite knew how to tell a great story. I feel that if you can tell a good story, people will want you. I moved into a top 20 market relatively quickly in my career. When I broke into a top 20 market, I thought, "Now what?"

6. What do you see as the future of producing content across various platforms?

It's changing, and it's changing very quickly. I just sat with Tom Mackin, the head of Rapala USA, and we were talking about this. I feel old. I can't keep up. Television is still a great medium. I think that there a lot of people who feel that newspapers and magazines are dying. Advertising is reflecting that. You have the Internet and social media, which are separate things in my mind.

The money still comes from television, not the Internet. I don't think that many people have figured out to have videos online and make money. There's a guy who has a video on how to tie the four fishing knots, and makes money from

Google. Some people are lucky that way.

On demand through the Internet is something that we're going to look at down the road. Instead of worrying what time the show will be on, you will be able to watch it online. We don't know what's going to happen with YouTube, Facebook and all those others.

I struggle with Facebook. I burn copious amounts of time because I feel that I need to, but I don't know that it's directly helping our company. I threatened to quit Facebook, but then I received comments from people who live vicariously through me.

7. What is your biggest catch?

I caught a 14-pound walleye through the ice on a barbless hook with 6-pound line up in Saskatchewan. That's the fish of a lifetime. Not just the fish, but that it was a barbless hook and 6-pound line.

I have caught some 45-inch pike up in Canada. I have as much fun seeing my 5-year-old catching sunfish and bass. That sensation is more profound. I have caught a lot of fish. When you get to pass along that passion to your kids, that's a big deal. Brady's five and Bennett is three. It's fun. That's my next chapter.

8. What are some of your favorite stories that you have covered in your career?

There are so many. Every time I go out the door, it seems like I meet wonderful people. I share a passion for the outdoors. The stories are great, the people are even better – literally every time that I go out. We just meet great people. The fun of this job is destinations and the people. It's the stories.

Everything we shoot.

I was working a booth at the ice fishing show in December. A couple of ninth graders wanted me to autograph their ball caps. I knew that I had a story when I met them. They go ice fishing every day. They want to be professional guides, but the biggest thing holding them back is that they don't have driver's licenses to go to the bait shop. It turned out to be a great story.

9. How can public relations professionals help you in your job? What are you looking for from them?

They are a key resource for us on many levels. Number one, helping us with story ideas. It's been a busy day. I was on the phone with someone from the state of South Dakota. He's a key resource on finding destinations, story ideas, money for sponsorships. Everywhere we go, they all have people working to promote a message. Those messages are all directly tied to what we do – travel, entertainment, natural resources. I deal with those folks daily.

It's the same for companies. Public relations and marketing folks can help with our advertising. They're kind of the conduit to the money at times. I love a lot of them and hate a few.

NONTRADITIONAL MEDIA PANEL REVEALS MANY SIMILARITIES

While the lines between traditional media, blogs and the social space have become increasingly blurred, many things remain constant.

Building relationships, following up and writing solid content still are important; even the telephone has a place in today's new media world.

"Social media is a great way to build relationships and interact, although email is the preferred way to pitch," said Jay Gabler of Minnesota Public Radio, one of the participants at a Minnesota PRSA nontraditional media panel hosted by Carmichael Lynch Spong in 2013.

Other members of the panel included: Rick Kupchella of BringMeTheNews; John Garland of the Heavy Table and the Growler Magazine; Missy Berggren (aka the "Marketing Mama") of WCG; and Bruno Bornsztein of Curbly, LLC.

Each participant has had success in his or her own right in the new media sphere. For instance, Kupchella's BringMeTheNews and related companies have created 100 jobs so far and have received $4.5 million in investments to date. Berggren has transformed her Marketing Mama blog from a way to initially express herself into an award-winning site.

Human interactions, whether good or difficult, still are important in new media.

"Any time I write about beer, inevitably someone is going to call me an idiot," said Garland. "People are passionate about beer."

Garland added that he is most impressed when restaurants take his Heavy Table reviews to heart and implement changes based on his feedback.

In terms of connecting with outlets that use freelancers, Gabler recommended pitching both editors and contributors. After all, the editors will be seeing the story eventually.

Another constant mentioned by participants is to get in touch with them in the way that they prefer to be contacted. "Getting phone calls from publicists and PR reps is always annoying and often works," said Gabler, quoting Twin Cities Daily Planet Editor Mary Turck.

In fact, Bornsztein recommended following up. That shows him the story – and his blog – are important.

While Bornsztein and Garland placed more of an emphasis on photos than the others, all panelists agreed that solid content and excellent relationships are important to successfully navigating today's new media world.

ENGAGING THE MEDIA IN A DIGITAL WORLD

In 2013 Business Wire and the Twin Cities chapter of National Investor Relations Institute hosted a media panel called "Engaging the Media in a Digital World: Social Media." Moderated by Bob Kleiber, the panel featured Kaeti Hinck of MinnPost, Dirk DeYoung of the Minneapolis/St. Paul Business Journal, David Fondler of St. Paul Pioneer Press and Todd Stone of Star Tribune.

Here is Brant's recap of the event.

1. Describe to what extent the journalist's job has become technology-driven.

Todd Stone (TS): "Social media has changed everything in a lot of ways." Stone added that the Star Tribune can reach more people through social media, and that "readers can engage us in so many more ways than before."

Kaeti Hinck (KH): "Social media gives reporters access to a wider array of contacts and tips." Hinck pointed out that MinnPost staff members check social media throughout the day.

Dirk DeYoung (DD): He starts his day at home editing the

"Morning Roundup" e-mail. "We don't save things for the print edition any more. The print edition is now for a deeper perspective." The Business Journal staffers use Twitter to get news tips; DeYoung highlighted how his reporters used LinkedIn recently to confirm that archivists were laid off at Target Corporation.

David Fondler (DF): "The Internet has made our jobs more challenging – the challenge is figuring out what is news." Fondler pointed out that Twitter is an excellent tool to help with reporting.

2. How do you like to be pitched by public relations professionals?

DF: "It's become much more of a fire hose – everyone thinks that their executive should be interviewed. We have to make fast-paced judgment calls to determine if we want to dedicate resources to follow a story."

DD: DeYoung said that he looks at least at the subject line of each e-mail, and that social media doesn't always get to him – so e-mail and phone can work better.

KH: "Social media provides the opportunity to learn about reporters and target pitches." She added, "If a company is doing good work, we're going to notice."

TS: He said that he likes to be contacted by e-mail or by phone call. "Use social media to get information out there, but contact reporters in the traditional ways."

3. What types of pressure are you getting to drive traffic to websites?

TS: "We want to engage more and more people."

KH: "Traffic remains important to us, although we're going after the right audience — not just any audience." Hinck added that she considers page views a dying metric.

DD: DeYoung said that The Business Journal constantly has goals to meet regarding growing page views and e-mail subscribers. He said that the publication's afternoon e-mail update has 16,000 subscribers. DeYoung said that the demand for videos is very strong, and that The Business Journal either shoots its own videos or uses videos from other sources.

DF: Fondler hasn't really felt pressure to drive traffic or get more page views. His team is constantly trying to keep headlines updated on the St. Paul Pioneer Press website. "Our mission is to get news to as many people as possible."

4. Do you see opportunities for media alliances?

DF: "I think it's a great idea."

DD: DeYoung mentioned that some other markets within The Business Journals chain have partnered with TV stations; the Minneapolis/St. Paul Business Journal has partnered with KMSP-TV and WCCO Radio. In addition, The Business Journals chain has a national partnership with Bloomberg.

KH: She said that MinnPost has a lot of partnerships.

TS: "Part of our mission and business model is to create unique content." He added, "Digital isn't pressuring us to partner with other organizations."

5. What are some social media must dos and never dos?

TS: Stone said to keep Twitter feeds more professional than

personal. "Be specific. Be precise." He added, "We use Twitter a lot as a reporting tool. Facebook provides us an opportunity to engage in the conversation."

KH: "Be smart – don't feed the trolls." Hinck also said to acknowledge any mistakes quickly, and to think before you retweet. "Choose one or two networks to focus on. Define your goals and measure those goals."

DD: "Don't be boring." DeYoung highlighted General Mills and Target as two brands that have excellent social media promoting blog content. DeYoung also recommended monitoring all streams of social media mentioning your company. He encouraged companies to make the Twitter handle easy to find on the website home page and in press releases.

DF: "Recognize that companies can't control the messages in social media." In regard to negative stories, he said, "Don't lie. Provide us with access. We'll make every opportunity to be fair." Some aspects of news criteria that Fondler mentioned were: Is it new? Is it unique? Does it touch a lot of people's lives? Is it local?

The panelists also mentioned that they still use wire services, such as Business Wire or PR Newswire.

MEET THE MEDIA: JOSH ROSENTHAL, CONTENT PRODUCER AT KSTP-TV

Authors' note: This Q&A originally appeared on the Skogrand PR Solutions Blog in 2013. Rosenthal now is a reporter at WTTG-TV in Washington, D.C.

1. Tell us a bit about your background.

I'm originally from Maryland, about 20 minutes outside of D.C. I wanted to become a journalist and went to the University of Maryland to major in journalism. I have been on air at stations in Gainesville, Fla., and Little Rock, Ark., before coming to the Twin Cities this year.

2. How have you adjusted to Minnesota weather?

So far, so good. I've actually lived here since January, so I feel that I already have experienced Minnesota weather. It's cold – I'm not going to lie. I feel that all of the great things about the Twin Cities outweigh the cold weather. I really love the Twin Cities.

3. How would you describe your approach to TV storytelling?

Well, it's important for people to remember that TV is a visual medium. I look for good, informative stories that our viewers want to learn about. It's important to find visual stories. It's important to find things within those stories for viewers to see.

4. Your stories almost have a bit of a theatrical element to them. How do you come up with ideas to demonstrate your stories?

It's a case-by-case thing. The day of the hail storm recently, I and the photographer tossed some ideas around. It's a storm damage story. Our morning reporter was working on covering a lot of trees down. We thought that covering hail damage would be good. Spotting downed trees is relatively easy, but finding hail damage is harder.

We decided to go to an auto body shop because we figured there would be people with hail damage there, and it was lines all day long.

We had our story, and we wanted to do something in the live shot rather than me just standing there. We asked the guy if he had any spare parts that were too far damaged to be salvaged. He had some car hoods. We then went to a sporting goods store, and bought some golf balls. I threw them against a car hood to demonstrate the damage that different size hail can do.

5. How has TV news changed during your career?

When I started a few years ago, social media was not nearly as large of a part of what we do. I can remember one of the first stories that I did in Gainesville, Fla. It was about a guy whose car was stolen and the police couldn't find it, and he posted on Facebook that his car was stolen. That wouldn't be a story today, because people post things like that all the time.

The story got better though, because one of his Facebook friends found the car. That wouldn't be a story today.

6. What do you see as the future of producing content across various platforms?

I'm not really sure where we're going. There's much more of an emphasis on hitting all platforms available to us. Now we're looking at how to tell the story on social media sites plus the KSTP-TV website.

7. What are some of your favorite stories that you have covered in Minnesota?

I did really like the hail story.

I produced a story a few months ago about an artist in Chanhassen who made his phone number public to everyone on the Internet. He asked people to call him about limitations or challenges that they faced. Maybe they got in an accident or had a rough time with their parents. He wrote the stories on a paper and then put it up on canvas. The way that he put the words from the stories on canvas resulted in one big picture. It was really interesting.

Any time you can tell a really visual story that makes people say, "Huh," and think about something, those are my favorites.

8. What are some of your favorite stories that you have covered in your career?

I have few notable ones. Severe weather stories tend to stick out. When I first got to Arkansas, it was a record year for flooding and tornadoes. That can be taxing too, though. It really wears on you as a person.

On a more fun note, in Gainesville, I interviewed Busta Rhymes and The Wiggles later on in the same day. That was interesting.

9. How can public relations professionals help you in your job? What are you looking for from them?

The toughest part of my job is coming to the table with stories for the newscast. I like to hear from public relations professionals. It helps when they have an understanding of what we do.

It also helps when there's a relationship there – when people develop a relationship ahead of time so I know my source. I love pitches with good stories and the visual component. Getting to know people can be very helpful – I appreciate calls from PR professionals.

SOCIAL NEWS GATHERING

Social media is playing an ever increasing role in news gathering, according to Dennis Powell, senior producer at ABC News. Powell spoke at a 2013 Minnesota PRSA-Social Media Breakfast Minneapolis/St. Paul event held at Best Buy headquarters.

For its coverage of Hurricane Sandy, Powell said that ABC News went through 300 pieces of social media. One piece that ABC News used was "HURRICANE SANDY 3 TREES FALL AND FIRE!!"[1] from YouTube.

"HootSuite is a wire desk of sources for a particular beat," said Powell.

While tweets can be published without permission, Powell emphasized the importance of authentication for other social media posts. For instance, ABC News will not run a YouTube video on air until it has the real name, phone number and e-mail address of the person who posted the video. This ensures that nothing fake is aired.

"Social media is an addition to the other news gathering tools," said Powell. When a news event happens, the ABC News

"1440 Social Media Desk" follows these tips in order to determine appropriate social media content:

- Put yourself in the place of the event.
- What would someone say?
- What would someone who knows someone say?
- Where would they say it?

Sources that the ABC News team uses as part of the social media news gathering toolkit include:

- Twitter search
- Twipho.net
- OpenStatusSearch.com
- Topsy.com
- Reddit
- Facebook
- ABC News staff

Not every event has social media commentary, though. For instance, Powell noted that the Newtown school shooting was not a social media moment.

MEET THE MEDIA: BILL HUDSON, STEPHANIE MARCH AND THOMAS LEE

At an Oct. 31, 2012, Minnesota Public Relations Society of America breakfast event, attendees learned a few tricks about connecting with the media while enjoying treats.

Moderator Dr. Michael Porter of the University of St. Thomas started out the panel discussion with an appropriate Halloween question, "What is the worst PR nightmare pitch that you have received?"

While Bill Hudson of WCCO-TV and Stephanie March of Mpls. St. Paul Magazine refused to comment, Thomas Lee of the Star Tribune shared his interesting story.

"My worst public relations nightmare was getting a pitch from a company promoting a product called Flatulence-D, with deals with farting after gastric bypass surgery," said Lee. "The person really had no clue what I wrote about."

Among the tips offered by Hudson, March and Lee were:

- Don't pitch more than one reporter at the same media outlet.

- Read the reporter's stories and what they have written about before pitching.
- Think in terms of both visuals and sound when pitching TV reporters.
- Learn the reporter's preferences in terms of connecting via e-mail or phone call.

The panelists agreed that media relations is about relationships.

"The best time to get in touch with a reporter is when you have nothing to pitch," said Lee. "You're in it for the long haul." Lee often uses ProfNet to find sources.

One attendee asked a question about connecting with reporters via social media. That turned out to be an individualized response. Lee primarily uses Twitter to find out about stories, while March is open to being pitched via Twitter. Hudson, however, isn't even on Twitter, so phone and e-mail are best for him.

How can public relations people stand out from the clutter? Attendees learned one trick: Send a handwritten note. It will get read.

A PLEASANT MINNESOTA SURPRISE FOR PRWEEK EDITOR-IN-CHIEF

In his first trip to Minnesota, Steve Barrett, editor-in-chief of PRWeek, learned that his perceptions of our state were quite different from the reality.

"I saw 'Fargo' and I know that Prince lived here," Barrett told a group of approximately 60 public relations professionals and students. "You have something green called grass, which we don't have in Manhattan."

At the 2012 Minnesota PRSA event hosted by Carmichael Lynch Spong, Barrett discussed what's driving agency growth, how PRWeek is changing, and how agencies are evolving.

Calling this "the most exciting time to be writing about PR and to be in the communications industry," Barrett said that integration is the way of the future for public relations agencies.

With skills perfectly suited to the modern media environment, PR professionals are integrating with the marketing and investor relations fields like never before.

Barrett pointed out that last year PR agencies were up 10

percent, while the national gross domestic product was up 1.7 percent. Social media and content generation are two of the keys to that growth – providing PR agencies a way to bypass traditional media and, in the case of social media, a cheaper way to connect with customers.

"Advertising is expensive," Barrett said. "As the saying goes, 'Fifty percent of advertising is effective, and we don't know which half.'"

This growth could lead to a billion-dollar agency possibly within the next five to 10 years.

Other aspects of this growth include globalization – particularly in Latin America and China – with agencies filling in the gaps to have a consistent offering around the world.

Three years ago, PRWeek changed its format to a monthly print publication, and continues to evolve.

"It's hard to peer into the crystal ball, although I can say we are integrating print with digital," Barrett said. "We have 22,000 Twitter followers and a YouTube channel. Our Tumblr blog is perfect for stories that wouldn't make the front page of the website."

Although there are no plans for a PRWeek iPad app, changes on tap for PRWeek include: more special events, possibly a more global perspective, and more webcasts.

In regard to agency trends, Barrett noted that agencies are getting to become choosier about their clients and in which RFPs they participate.

He added that measurement continues to be the holy grail. Agencies – and corporations – are building their own analytics tools but are secretive about it because of the inherent competitive advantage.

Speaking of transparency, Barrett also touched on the mistakes that caused the CEO of Yahoo to resign, as well as Best Buy's CEO and founder to give up their positions.

"Everything is transparent these days," Barrett said. "You're playing Russian roulette if you think that something isn't going to come out."

Feel free to come back to Minnesota anytime, Steve. Maybe you can experience the joy of a good snowball fight or the thrill of catching a big walleye while ice fishing.

PART FOUR
PUBLIC RELATIONS CASE STUDIES

TYLENOL

To millions, Tylenol is an effective over-the-counter pain reliever. In public relations circles, however, the 1982 Tylenol recall represents the epitome of crisis communications.

At that time, Tylenol was a very important product to its manufacturer, Johnson & Johnson. Tylenol represented 33 percent of the company's year-to-year profit growth and outsold the next four leading painkillers combined.

In fall 1982, a horrible crisis happened. Someone replaced Tylenol Extra-Strength capsules with cyanide-laced capsules, resealed the packages and placed them back on the shelves of at least six pharmacies and grocery stores in the Chicago area. Seven people died after consuming the tainted capsules.

Robert Andrews, assistant director for public relations at Johnson & Johnson at the time, is quoted in Dieudonnée ten Berge's book "The First 24 Hours: A Comprehensive Guide to Successful Crisis Management," on how the company initially heard the news: "We got a call from a Chicago news reporter. He told us that the medical examiner there had just given a press conference saying that people were dying from poisoned Tylenol. He wanted our comment. As it was the first knowledge we had here in this department, we told him we knew nothing about it. In that first call we learned more from the reporter than he did from us."

Johnson & Johnson Chairman James Burke swiftly formed a seven-member strategy team, guiding them to answer two questions: "How do we protect the people?" and "How do we save the product?"

Johnson & Johnson immediately used media relations to alert consumers not to take Tylenol – and to not resume until the extent of the tampering was determined. The company also stopped producing and advertising Tylenol, and withdrew the product from store shelves in the Chicago area.

Two more contaminated bottles were discovered, and Johnson & Johnson took the major step of ordering a national recall of Tylenol.

The national recall, despite a small chance of discovering more cyanide-laced capsules, demonstrated the company's commitment to public safety. As a result, Johnson & Johnson was perceived as a victim.

In addition to the national media alert and interviews, Johnson & Johnson:

- Established a 1-800 hotline for consumers to call,
- Created a toll-free line for the media to call and receive recorded messages with the latest statements on the crisis,
- Held press conferences at the corporate headquarters, and
- Set up a live satellite feed to the New York metro area.

At one of the press conferences, Johnson & Johnson revealed the new Tylenol triple safety seal packaging – a glued box, a plastic seal over the neck of the bottle, and a foil seal over the mouth of the bottle.

The Tylenol crisis was a major nationwide news story, with 90 percent of Americans having heard of the news in the first week. Two clipping services found more than 125,000 news stories on the crisis.

Beyond the recall and changing product packaging, Johnson & Johnson provided the victims' families counseling and financial assistance – even though the company was not responsible for the tampering.

The crisis shaped Johnson & Johnson's public relations strategy from a passive to proactive approach.

By deftly handling the Tylenol crisis, Johnson & Johnson completely recovered the market share lost during the crisis and reestablished Tylenol as one of the most trusted over-the-counter consumer products.

NESTLE INFANT FORMULA

Infant formula is one of the products that helped create food conglomerate Nestlé when, in 1867, Swiss pharmacist Henri Nestlé mixed together a liquid food from cow's milk, wheat flour, and sugar for a neighbor's baby who wouldn't nurse.

Infant formula also is the reason for a boycott against the company, launched in Minneapolis in 1977.

The roots of the boycott started in 1974, when the British organization War on Want published a booklet called "The Baby Killer." The booklet was widely distributed and translated into several languages. As a result, many church-related groups joined against Nestlé.

Nestlé responded by suing the publisher of the German-language translation, Third World Action Group, for libel. While Nestlé won the two-year trial, the defendants were fined only $400 and the judge told Nestlé that it "must modify its publicity methods fundamentally."

The topic of analyzing the marketing of breast milk substitutes in developing countries continued to gain traction with a U.S. Senate public hearing as well as WHO and UNICEF hosting an international meeting.

In 1981, The New York Times **published a lengthy article**[1] on infant formula use in developing countries.

Problems when mothers of infants in developing countries switch to formula include: disease because of contaminated water; lack of means to sterilize water; and diluting formula to make it last longer.

Around the same time as the 1981 article, research demonstrated that breastfeeding is healthier for babies.

Nestlé met with boycott coordinators in 1984, and the boycott was suspended when the company agreed to adhere to the World Health Assembly's International Code of Marketing of Breast-milk Substitutes. However, the boycott resumed in 1989 when the **International Baby Food Action Network** alleged that formula companies were providing free and low-cost supplies to hospitals in developing countries.

Even though Nestlé issued guidelines for mothers on how and when to give babies formula as well as revamping its marketing materials, the boycott still exists today and even has expanded.

TARGET DATA BREACH

In analyzing the 2013 Target data breach, I (Brant) will use the eight laws of crisis communications that Jack Yeo and John Brooks presented at the 2012 PRSA Midwest District Conference in Chicago:

1. **Protecting reputation is not about the crisis, but rather how you handle it.** Target used many methods of responding to the crisis, including full-page newspaper ads in the nation's top 50 markets. In addition, Target sent an e-mail from CEO Gregg Steinhafel explaining the breach, apologizing and offering free credit monitoring services. (Unfortunately, many customers were leery of the e-mails.) Steinhafel also appeared on CNBC on Jan. 13, 2014, where he said, "We are responsible, we're accountable for all of it, and we want to make that crystal clear to everybody that's shopped in our store. They have zero liability."
2. **Be aware of the world around you.** Ensuring that call centers and stores had accurate information took a while for Target — specifically four days. In the CNBC interview, Steinhafel said, "Part of that timetable all along was for us to make that announcement on day

four, and we were working around the clock to prepare our stores. We want guests that come in, once they hear that news, we want to be able to answer their questions, and we want our call centers to function appropriately."
3. **There is no excuse for not planning.** Data breaches have become increasingly common among retailers and other companies. If Target had a crisis response manual (I'm not sure if they do or not), a data breach should definitely have been one of the main situations to prepare for.
4. **A swift response is required.** This is the area in which Target is receiving the most criticism. Star Tribune columnist Lee Schafer describes Target's public relations as "too slow, too cautious" in this article.[1] He makes a very valid point that on Dec. 18, 2013, the same day computer security blogger Brian Krebs posted a story stating that Target was confronting a security breach, the company instead issued a news release[2] about last-minute holiday season deals. Target didn't issue a news release[3] about the data breach until the next day. (The company first learned of the breach on Dec. 15.) In addition, Steinhafel wasn't made available for a public statement for more than three weeks.
5. **Understand the impact of today's digital democracy.** Target developed a page on its website with response and resources related to the data breach, including videos featuring Steinhafel. The retailer monitored what was being said on social media, even mentioning in a Jan. 15, 2014, tweet, "We're listening & noticing tweets about data breach emails."[4] The content of social media posts changed from holiday cheer to the data breach on Dec. 19, the same day that the company publicly confirmed that credit and debit card information may have been exposed.

6. **Always operate with transparency.** This is another area in which target is taking heat. In a Jan. 14, 2014, Star Tribune article[5] that featured highlights from Steinhafel's CNBC interview, reporter Adam Belz wrote that Target's CEO declined to be interviewed by the hometown newspaper. In addition, crisis management consultant Jon Austin made the point in the same article that "He (Steinhafel) was very good, he was very credible, he was very practiced, he stayed on message ... but he didn't say anything that he couldn't have said on Dec. 19."
7. **Never stand alone.** Third-party influencers didn't really make an appearance in the data breach timeline until Target chief financial officer John Mulligan spoke in front of a Senate panel.[6] Minnesota Senators Amy Klobuchar and Al Franken, both members of the Judiciary Committee, made statements in support of Target on the issue. "When we push cyberbills, we get push back [from industry and technology groups]," Klobuchar said. "We have learned from this data breach that we can no longer do nothing." Franken added that card technology needs to be updated.
8. **Never forget to rebuild.** Target has been working hard to rebuild the trust with its guests. The CEO could be more visible in the media however.

If I were to grade Target's response to this issue, I would give the company an "A-." The company understood the importance of maintaining the confidence of its customers. However, the delay in communicating and not making the CEO available for a public statement for more than three weeks diminished the effectiveness of Target's crisis response.

TOXIC SHOCK SYNDROME

Let's start with a brief history of the tampon. While tampon-like solutions have been around for centuries, none met the needs of women entering the 20th century workplace until the modern tampon was invented in 1936 by a Denver physician named Earle Haas.

Haas sold his patent to Tampax Incorporated, and before long, 90 percent of all tampon users relied on Tampax.

Author Laurie Garrett points out in her book *The Coming Plague* that, "though history showed that other approaches to the bleeding problem had been associated with elevated risks of some infectious diseases, commercial tampons were sold without any more regulation than hammers or soap."[1]

With the huge baby boomer market of young women that came along in the 1970s, four multinational corporations (The Kimberly-Clark Corporation, Procter & Gamble, Playtex, and Johnson & Johnson) decided to enter the tampon market.

Competition got more intense when, in the mid-1970s, the National Association of Broadcasters lifted its longtime ban on radio and television advertising of tampons. The two key focal points in tampon ads were comfort and security.

Absorbency became a way to chip away at Tampax's domination of the market, and a breakthrough came in 1974 when Procter & Gamble engineers developed a product based not on cotton and cardboard but on polyester fibers and plastic. The use of synthetic fibers provided a practically unlimited number of ways to vary the shape and relative absorbency of tampons.

In 1979, Procter & Gamble launched Rely, a synthetic tampon that could absorb nearly 20 times its own weight in fluids. The Rely tampon was comprised of highly compressed beads of, alternately, polyester and carboxymethyl cellulose. Rely tampons became popular quite quickly thanks to a huge advertising campaign and its superabsorbency.

The superabsorbency had issues, though: some women had pain when the tampon was removed, residue of synthetic pieces was left behind in some instances, and other women needed medical assistance to get the tampon removed because it became too big.

Around 1979 to early 1980, some states started reporting higher instances of Toxic Shock Syndrome (TSS), an illness marked by a fever greater than 102 °F, red rashes, a marked drop in blood pressure, vomiting, and more. A common denominator of most of the TSS cases was that most of the patients were menstruating females.

According to Garrett's book *The Coming Plague*, news coverage of TSS cases was "terrifying":

- "Teenager dies of tampon use. Details at eleven!"
- "Toxic Shock Syndrome survivor tells her story tonight on Eyewitness News."
- "Centers for Disease Control warning women to

beware of tampons. Stay tuned for more!"²

The outbreaks of TSS notably were clustered in Wisconsin and Minnesota. Most of the female TSS cases involved individuals who used superabsorbent tampons. On Sept. 19, 1980, the Centers for Disease Control (CDC) released a report taking aim at Rely tampons, stating that a controlled study showed that other brands had a much lower incidence of TSS.

Procter & Gamble then made a bold move, according to *The Coming Plague*:

> On September 22, just days after the release of the CDC report, Procter & Gamble voluntarily removed Rely from the marketplace. And they went a step further: together with the Food and Drug Administration, the company designed a massive ad campaign telling women not to use their product. The campaign, which began October 6, ran on network television and radio and in over 1,200 newspapers nationwide for four weeks. The FDA, meanwhile, urged women to get rid of their existing supplies of Rely, and recalled inventories of the product from stores nationwide.³

Said Procter & Gamble company representative at the time, Marjorie Bradford, "Procter & Gamble makes over 88 consumer brands of household and hygiene products. We must maintain a reputation for safe and effective products."

Some non-CDC scientists were unsure of the CDC's position, though.

Public hearings were held and the first tampon regulations were issued.

Something strange happened in Minnesota: four weeks after the Rely tampons went off the market, a surge in TSS cases occurred. In addition, Rely was never sold in Connecticut, yet the state still had TSS cases.

A scientist from UCLA, Patrick Schlievert, discovered that a staphylococcal poison caused TSS. The menstrual cycle provided the ideal vehicle for hosting bacteria and a tampon provided a great growth surface.

TSS faded from media headlines as cases declined. Why the geographic cluster in Wisconsin and Minnesota, though? Turns out that TSS had the highest incidence among people of Scandinavian and German heritage.

In the end, the CDC discovered that "tampon absorbency was strongly correlated with the risk of contracting TSS, though the chemical content of the tampons was not."

Because of the incident, tampon boxes now have messages about TSS and the terms related to absorbency were standardized. Procter & Gamble still has a sterling reputation.

CHIPOTLE E. COLI AND NOROVIRUS OUTBREAK

In late October 2015, nearly two dozen people reported having an E. coli infection after eating at Chipotle restaurants in the Pacific Northwest. Shortly after the incident, Chipotle closed 43 restaurants in the surrounding area due to food safety concerns. Although only eight restaurants were found to be contaminated, Chipotle closed additional locations as a precaution.

In the days after the outbreak, Chipotle was applauded for its positive outreach. The restaurant chain released an FAQ, welcomed questions regarding the outbreak and remained transparent as the issue progressed. Outlets wrote articles applauding the positive PR strategy following the outbreak. A couple weeks later, Chipotle made headlines again when its co-CEOs appeared publicly disjointed.

In addition to crisis communications, leaders need to be on the same page when a crisis hits. According to Fortune,[1] Chipotle co-CEO Monty Moran recently spoke at an industry conference for investors and shifted blame from Chipotle to the Centers for Disease Control and Prevention (CDC). Instead of moving the conversation forward, Moran complained about the sensationalized headlines. However true he may be, it left loyal

Chipotle goers with a bad taste in their mouth.

Steve Ells, Chipotle's founder, chairman and co-CEO, took another approach by running a letter from him outlining the chain's comprehensive food safety plan in major daily newspapers. In the Dec. 16 letter, Ells mentioned the chain has hired outside food safety consultants to look at the food safety standards and is implementing high-resolution sampling and testing that is "unprecedented in the restaurant industry" to prevent contaminants such as E. coli.

Ells gets PR brownie points for his statement, but the disunity between him and Moran took away from Ells' overall message. The lesson we can learn from Chipotle's recent outbreak is the need for unified leadership and positive reactive PR.

Despite the company's 20 percent dip in share price, it's not likely that Chipotle's recent blunders will keep the company out of the game for long. Chipotle is still steadily gaining popularity and continues to develop new locations. In fact, the line at the Chipotle near me (Aliki) in Minneapolis still has its continuous line out the door.

NOTES

Benefits of Media Coverage
1. "Further Decline in Credibility Ratings for Most News Organizations," Pew Research Center, Aug. 16, 2012, http://www.people-press.org/2012/08/16/further-decline-in-credibility-ratings-for-most-news-organizations/
2. "Press Widely Criticized, But Trusted More than Other Information Sources," Pew Research Center, Sept. 22, 2011, http://www.people-press.org/2011/09/22/press-widely-criticized-but-trusted-more-than-other-institutions/

When to Do Media Relations: Company Announcement
1. Antony Leather, "The iPhone 7: Five Reasons I Would and Wouldn't Buy It," Forbes, June 3, 2016, https://www.forbes.com/sites/antonyleather/2016/06/03/the-iphone-7-five-reasons-i-would-and-wouldnt-buy-it/#64d2cd3852bd

When to Do Media Relations: Promoting an Event

NOTES

1. Gail Knox, "Relay For Life headed for Mpls. skyways," KARE11, April 27, 2016, https://www.kare11.com/article/entertainment/television/programs/kare-11-news-at-11/relay-for-life-headed-for-mplsskyways/156232895

When to Do Media Relations: Trending News Stories

1. tictac. (2016, Oct. 8). "Tic Tac respects all women. We find the recent statements and behavior completely inappropriate and unacceptable." [Twitter post]. Retrieved from https://twitter.com/tictac/status/785373622068187136
2. Julia Reinstein, "Tic Tac — Yes, Tic Tac — Has Broken Its Silence On That Trump Video," BuzzFeed News, Oct. 8, 2016, https://www.buzzfeednews.com/article/juliareinstein/woke-kings-of-freshness#.wyOqmOBzL

When to Do Media Relations: Tell the Big Picture

1. Mark Reilly, "Why Glam Doll Donuts is hoarding Sriracha," Minneapolis/St. Paul Business Journal, Nov. 25, 2013, https://www.bizjournals.com/twincities/morning_roundup/2013/11/why-glam-doll-donuts-is-hoarding.html

When to Do Media Relations: Media Coverage Opportunities

1. Arielle Calderon, "We Tried Low-Cal Ice Creams And Compared Them To Häagen-Dazs," BuzzFeed News, March 11, 2016, https://www.buzzfeed.com/ariellecalderon/low-cal-ice-cream-taste-test

Understanding the Basics of SEO for Public Relations

1. Marta Kagan, "100 Awesome Marketing Stats, Charts, & Graphs," HubSpot, https://blog.hubspot.com/blog/tabid/6307/bid/14416/100-Awesome-Marketing-Stats-Charts-Graphs-Data.aspx
2. Brant Skogrand, APR, and Chris Peterson, "If they can find it, they will come: Optimizing your online pressroom," TACTICS, March 2009, http://skograndpr.com/wp-content/uploads/2014/10/Optimizing_online.pdf

How to Leverage Media Coverage

1. Brant Skogrand, APR, and Chris Peterson, "If they can find it, they will come: Optimizing your online pressroom," TACTICS, March 2009, http://skograndpr.com/wp-content/uploads/2014/10/Optimizing_online.pdf

Church Public Relations

1. Lannie Walker, "Christian rock band's first album is iTunes hit," Star Tribune, April 14, 2013, http://www.startribune.com/christian-rockers-itunes-success-helps-church-with-apple-valley-branch/202860461/

Beyond the Press Release: Developing Other Media Materials

1. Aliki Vrohidis, "Six public relations trends for 2016," Skogrand PR Solutions Blog, Jan. 8, 2016, https://skograndpr.com/2016/01/08/five-public-relations-trends-for-2016/
2. Ezra Fishman, "How Long Should Your Next Video Be?" Wistia, July 5, 2016, https://wistia.com/learn/marketing/optimal-video-length

Why Influencer Marketing Is Important

1. "Influencer Marketing Study," Tomoson Blog, https://www.tomoson.com/blog/influencer-marketing-

study/
2. Andrew Perrin, "Social Media Usage: 2005-2015," Pew Research Center, Oct. 8, 2015, https://www.pewinternet.org/2015/10/08/social-networking-usage-2005-2015/
3. "Consumer Trust in Online, Social and Mobile Advertising Grows," The Nielsen Company, April 11, 2012, https://www.nielsen.com/us/en/insights/article/2012/consumer-trust-in-online-social-and-mobile-advertising-grows/

Influencer Marketing Best Practices

1. "2019 Edelman Trust Barometer," Edelman, Jan. 20, 2019, www.edelman.com/trust-barometer
2. Kimberlee Morrison, "Why Influencer Marketing is the New Content King [Infographic]," Adweek, April 3, 2015, www.adweek.com/digital/why-influencer-marketing-is-the-new-content-king-infographic/
3. "The State of Influencer Marketing 2019 : Benchmark Report [+Infographic]," Influencer Marketing Hub, May 28, 2019, https://influencermarketinghub.com/influencer-marketing-2019-benchmark-report/
4. Eileen Brown, "Influencer marketing spending is on the rise," ZDNet, June 14, 2019, www.zdnet.com/article/influencer-marketing-spending-is-on-the-rise-according-to-new-reports/

Brands That Have Succeeded with Influencer Marketing

1. Ashley Karhoff, "5 Creative Influencer Campaigns to Inspire Content Marketers," NewsCred Insights, Aug. 18, 2016, https://insights.newscred.com/influencer-campaigns-content-marketers/
2. Ibid.

3. Ibid.
4. Lisa Furgison, "How 'Boxed Water' Combined Influencer and Cause Marketing," IZEA, Feb. 29, 2016, https://insights.newscred.com/influencer-campaigns-content-marketers/

Social News Gathering

1. imasharky, "HURRICANE SANDY 3 TREES FALL AND FIRE!!," YouTube, Oct. 29, 2012, https://www.youtube.com/watch?v=OZlZUsqkVx8&feature=youtu.be

Nestlé Infant Formula

1. Stephen Solomon, "The Controversy Over Infant Formula," The New York Times, Dec. 6, 1981, https://www.nytimes.com/1981/12/06/magazine/the-controversy-over-infant-formula.html?pagewanted=all

Target Data Breach

1. Lee Schafer, "Target's response was too slow, too cautious," Star Tribune, Jan. 19, 2014, http://www.startribune.com/schafer-target-s-response-was-too-slow-too-cautious/240894901/
2. Target Corporation (2013). "Target Unveils Last-Minute Deals in Final Stretch of Strong Holiday Season." [Online] Available at: https://corporate.target.com/press/releases/2013/12/target-unveils-last-minute-deals-in-final-stretch [Accessed June 24, 2019].
3. Target Corporation (2013). "Target Confirms Unauthorized Access to Payment Card Data in U.S. Stores." [Online] Available at: https://corporate.target.com/press/releases/2013/12/target-confirms-unauthorized-access-to-payment-car [Accessed June 24, 2019].

4. Target Corporation. (2014, Jan. 15). "We're listening & noticing tweets about data breach emails. Official Target communication can be confirmed here: http://tgt.biz/pci" [Twitter post]. Retrieved from https://twitter.com/target/status/423652845779316737
5. Adam Belz, "Target seeks to reassure customers," Star Tribune, Jan. 14, 2014, http://www.startribune.com/jan-14-target-ceo-seeks-to-reassure-customers/240030301/
6. Jim Spencer, "Target gives new details on data theft to senators," Star Tribune, Feb. 5, 2014, http://www.startribune.com/feb-4-target-gives-new-details-on-data-theft/243508791/

Toxic Shock Syndrome

1. Garrett, L. (1994). Feminine Hygiene (As Debated, Mostly, by Men). In *The Coming Plague* (p. 392). New York, NY: Farrar, Straus and Giroux.
2. Ibid., 397.
3. Ibid., 398.

Chipotle E. Coli and Norovirus Outbreak

1. Ben Geier, "Here's How Chipotle Is Responding Its E. Coli Crisis," Fortune, Nov. 3, 2015, http://fortune.com/2015/11/03/heres-how-chipotle-is-responding-its-e-coli-crisis/

ABOUT THE AUTHORS

Brant Skogrand, APR, MBC, CPPM, is assistant news editor at the University of St. Thomas in St. Paul, Minnesota. He's also the chief communications officer of Skogrand PR Solutions, LLC (www.skograndpr.com), a public relations, social media and search engine optimization firm. He is Accredited in Public Relations, a Certified Master of Social Media and is certified in search engine marketing. He has a bachelor's degree in journalism from the University of Minnesota and a master's degree in business communication from the University of St. Thomas. Brant has served as the chair of the Midwest district and as president of the Minnesota chapter of the Public Relations Society of America. He also is the author of the books *Maynard's Memories*, *19 Tips for Successful Public Relations*, and *From Fringe Party to Serious Contender*. Brant posts regularly to the Skogrand PR Solutions Blog (www.skograndpr.com/blog). He resides in Apple Valley, Minnesota, with his wife, son and calico cat.

Photo credit: Mark Brown/University of St. Thomas

Kate Makowski received her bachelor's degree in professional strategic communications from the University of Minnesota. Since graduating, she's worked in newsletter editing, content planning, social media strategy and digital ads. In her spare time, Kate enjoys exploring new breweries, attending bar trivia, performing (singing) at local venues, and spending time with her beloved cat, Weasley.

Aliki Vrohidis is a public relations specialist at Andersen Corporation with successful experience helping build company reputation, expanding brand awareness, supporting strategic business initiatives through media relations, influencer engagement and content development. Aliki specializes in establishing and managing influencer partnerships including identifying influencers, negotiating terms, amplifying content and tracking results. Aliki earned a Bachelor of Arts in strategic communications and business management from the University of Minnesota. Aliki enjoys trying new restaurants, listening to true crime podcasts and spending time with her golden retriever, Birdie.

PROMOTING YOUR BUSINESS

How to Harness the Power of Media Relations and Influencer Marketing

Brant Skogrand, APR, MBC, CPPM

with Kate Makowski and Aliki Vrohidis

Copyright © 2019 Brant Skogrand, Kate Makowski and Aliki Vrohidis.

All rights reserved. This book is protected by the copyright laws of the United States of America. This book may not be copied or reprinted for commercial gain or profit.

The publisher is not responsible for websites (or their content) that are not owned by the publisher.

Cover design: Patty Skogrand

www.ingramcontent.com/pod-product-compliance
Lightning Source LLC
Chambersburg PA
CBHW030630220526
45463CB00004B/1476